# THE QUILTED
# GARDEN

## JANE A. SASSAMAN

C&T PUBLISHING

Copyright © 2000 Jane A. Sassaman
Editor: Annie Nelson
Technical Editor: Lynn Koolish
Copyeditor: Steven Cook
Book and Cover Design: Aliza Kahn
Front Cover Image: Detail of *Garden Triptych*, 12" x 12", ©1999
Back Cover Image: *Willow*, 75" x 75", ©1996
Production Direction: Kathy Lee
Photography credits as noted per image. All nature
photography, home and studio shots, process shots,
and author photo by Gregory Gantner. To contact Judy
Smith-Kressley: www.JSKphotoart.com.

Attention Teachers:
C&T Publishing, Inc. encourages you to use this book as a
text for teaching. Contact us at 800-284-1114 or
www.ctpub.com for more information about the C&T
Teachers Program.

We take great care to ensure that the information included
in this book is accurate and presented in good faith, but no
warranty is provided nor results guaranteed. Since we have
no control over the choice of materials or procedures used,
neither the authors nor C&T Publishing, Inc. shall have any
liability to any person or entity with respect to any loss or
damage caused directly or indirectly by the information
contained in this book.

**Library of Congress Cataloging-in-Publication Data**
Sassaman, Jane A.
    The quilted garden : design & make nature inspired
    quilts / Jane A. Sassaman.
        p. cm.
Includes bibliographical references (p.   ) and index.
    ISBN 1-57120-103-3 (paper trade)
1. Appliqué. 2. Quilts--Design. 3. Embroidery, Machine. I. Title.
TT779 .S27 2000
746.46'041--dc21
                                    99-050954

Trademarked (™) and Registered Trademarked (®) names
are used throughout this book. Rather than use the symbols with every occurrence of a trademark and registered
trademark name, we have only used the symbol the first
time the product appears. We are using the names only in
an editorial fashion and to the benefit of the owner, with
no intention of infringement.

Published by C&T Publishing, Inc.
P.O. Box 1456
Lafayette, California 94549

Printed in Hong Kong
10  9  8  7  6  5  4  3  2  1

# TABLE OF CONTENTS

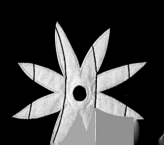

# DEDICATION

This book was written to encourage budding quilt artists to find their own voice through thoughtful design and careful craftsmanship.

# APPRECIATION

I would like to acknowledge my debt to the originals, the men and women who recognized the expressive potential of quilts and made the commitment to communicate with fabric and threads. Their passion pioneered a contemporary art movement in the face of great odds. These artists made innovations that went beyond the techniques and subjects of quilting, their hard work has established an international network for exhibiting, promoting, and learning about contemporary quiltmaking.

They have created a well-paved career path for those of us who have aspired to follow their vision. The career opportunities are still expanding, thanks to the adventurous efforts of the first wave art quilters. As the foremost art quilters are recognized as artists outside the insular world of quilting, the world of the second wave quilter expands simultaneously. I am thankful for the courageous efforts of my quilting mentors. They created a light for me to steer toward, and every day I benefit from their expertise, experience, and generosity.

I would also like to recognize the students who continuously amaze me with their kindness and support. Quilting is a very solitary art. It is only when I go out into the world as a teacher that I am surprised to find so many people are paying attention to the work I have been doing. It is gratifying to realize that others have been as excited by the shapes and colors that have entertained me for hours in the studio.

My students have been enthusiastic and encouraging. They, more than anyone, convinced me to put together this book. I come home from classes sparked with inspiration and recharged to get down to work. Teaching has challenged me to put my ideas into words, a job I was reluctant to encounter, but one which has pushed me to discover new talents and expand my dreams.

Thanks to C&T for the opportunity to compile twenty years of exploration and energy into a single volume, and to Judy Smith-Kressley for coming to my rescue at the eleventh hour.

I wish to thank Rob and Sandra Adams for entrusting me with their collection of original prints by some of the masters of decorative art in the early-twentieth century. It was a thrill to be able to absorb them in person.

And thanks to Inez Howard for loaning me the wonderful volume from her inspired collection of wonders.

I will always be grateful to my parents, the engineer and the perfectionist, for their quiet encouragement and proud promotion of my work. "The harder I work the luckier I get."

I am also thankful to Ellen and Robert Gantner for welcoming me into the fold so many years ago and for respecting the convoluted path we have chosen to travel.

Big thanks go to Oliver and Willow, too, for having patience with a mom who would rather quilt than make dinner. You have inspired me more than you know.

And most importantly, I would like to thank Greg, the most passionate man I know, for his enthusiastic support of our partnership. Your zeal for life and natural curiosity has enriched us all and kept us on our toes.

He who works with his hands is a laborer. He who works

with his hands, head and his heart is an artist. —St. Francis of Assisi

# PREFACE

*Every day I give thanks that I am able to do what I love. Quiltmaking provides all of the elements that satisfy my soul: color, bold designs, craftsmanship, fabric, and a wonderful degree of self-autonomy.*

*I love fabric. It's tactile and very personal. I feel an intimacy with fabric and thread that nothing else provides. It is a delicate, yet potentially powerful, medium. Fabric is the primary language through which my ideas are translated.*

*In working with colorful fabrics cut into dramatic shapes, I attempt to express the energy and mystery of our amazing universe—from the miraculous beauty of a single blossom to the complicated powers of the soul.*

*I want to dazzle the viewer, to snap them out of a mundane routine, and remind them that they are a part of a bigger "cosmic picture." I want the viewer to be as excited by the contrasting shapes and colors as I am when the piece is coming to life. I hope this joy and enthusiasm radiates from every quilt. Likewise, I hope the images in this book encourage your own pursuit of wonder and ignite your creative powers.*

◄ *Tree of Life: Summer*, 24½" x 39½",
©1995, private collection.

Photo by Judy Smith-Kressley.

& influences

# BEGINNING

I have always wanted to be an artist. In fact, I never felt the need to decide what to "be"; it was already determined. I came into this life with a prepacked satchel of color preferences, a magnetic attraction toward certain shapes, and a leaning toward decorative design.

By the age of twelve, I also realized that I wanted to be the master of a medium (preferably something rare and arcane) that required fine skill and practice. This realization came after seeing a film clip, probably in a commercial, showing a specially-trained calligrapher painting an ornate manuscript letter. She was divinely focused on that mystical design as she stroked it with a fine brush. "That's for me!" I thought. I wanted to experience the same intense devotion, precision, and concentration while making objects of extraordinary beauty and individuality.

I didn't know where this desire would lead, but by exploring every medium available, I knew I was on the proper path. I shared my artistic goals with my best friend in grade school. Together, we pursued every opportunity for artistic advancement: summer classes, contests, and forever drawing and making things.

Our first patron was the wonderfully eccentric woman who lived between our houses. She and her husband owned the local paint and decorating store. She was eccentric to us because her home was full of bizarre artwork and exotic artifacts that she inherited from her father, who spent his life as a missionary in China.

She also had a large yard like none other. It was natural, undisciplined, and mysterious. Her yard was full of trees and flowers that inhabited every nook and cranny. It was wild and wonderful and visited by interesting people. And on top of it all, she tended her garden in her slip at the crack of dawn!

This curious woman kept us supplied with art materials—paint, brushes, books, canvas board, charcoal—things that we would never have been exposed to at that age. She introduced us to a wider world, a world that went beyond a normal Midwestern, middle-class existence. She surrounded herself with beauty and recognized us for our potential beauty, too. Her recognition gave us our early identities as artists.

At home, my parents also encouraged my artistic activities. They finished a basement room and furnished it with a drawing table and stereo. It was my refuge. I was quite happy there drawing, painting, compiling books of inspirational pictures, and dreaming. I spent so much time in my yellow basement studio that my mother began calling me "The Mole" and worrying about my inactive social life. But I was in the realm of all possibilities and content. I was planning my future.

Jane as a high school student in 1970.

*Photo by Dorothy Gugel.*

I was encouraged further by high school art teachers. My free time at school was spent in the art classroom, experimenting with ceramics, weaving, and painting. Craftsmanship added extra appeal to any medium. When I went to college, it was only natural that I gravitated toward applied art and settled into textile and jewelry design. Through these classes and others, I was introduced to still more exotic worlds. From there, my curiosity set me on a course of self-education.

Magazines such as *Vogue* and *Harper's Bazaar* exposed me to fashion illustration. From these pages I discovered a world of opulence, where people live for beautiful details and extraordinary artistry and craftsmanship. It was here that I first saw the elegant, pleated satin Fortuny gowns, trimmed with tiny beads at every seam, and the unforgettable home of Gloria Vanderbilt, a jewel box of sumptuous pattern, lined with quilts on the floors, walls, doors, and ceilings. The elegance and extravagance was breathtaking. To know that such unearthly beauty could exist if you had the courage and vision to create it (or the money to buy it) was a new idea.

Although I loved art history classes, they frustrated me because of their lack of detail. Consequently, I spent many hours in the college library trying to fill those empty spaces. In the library I discovered wonderful things. I found an original set of hand-printed patterns by Seguy, an early twentieth-century French designer of decoration. He is especially known for his designs inspired by insects and flowers. Because these pages were hand printed, the layers of color had a relief quality, and by studying these plates, I was able to determine the sequence of printing. Seguy is still one of my favorite designers. Being able to study his designs in their original form was invaluable.

A painting I did in high school. Note the similarity to my current work: bright solid colors and pattern.

Seguy book cover

The artist William Morris also influenced my budding concepts of craftsmanship and artistic integrity. He was one of many Victorian artists offended by the progress of the Industrial Age. Instead, they extolled the romanticized ideals of Gothic poetry, architecture, and craftsmanship.

Supporters of the Arts and Crafts Movement also believed that satisfying handwork was an antidote for a life stripped of self-expression by mechanization and urbanization. Consequently, they praised the craftsman as a heroic, even glamorous, individual with the noble purpose of beautifying and civilizing his or her world.

As the pivotal figure in the Arts and Crafts Movement, William Morris pioneered the revival of many craft techniques and promoted the serious study of nature. He encouraged artists to become involved in decorative work. Artists began designing rugs, wallpaper, jewelry, ceramics, glass, and furniture. The Arts and Crafts Movement set in motion an artistic revolution whose influence is still strong at the beginning of the twenty-first century.

*Corncockle* chintz by William Morris, 1883.

Photo courtesy of William Morris Designs and Patterns, Norah Gillow, Crescent Books.

Seguy book plate

This romantic ideal of the artist/craftsman was very appealing to me, and I fell in line easily with their philosophy. Obviously, I was not the only one feeling this way in the '60s and '70s. The slick, plastic, industrial twentieth century produced many other people who wanted to find individual expression within the mass-produced contemporary society. This movement was supported by art schools and colleges with an international mix of sophisticated and educated crafts teachers.

A book called *Objects USA* by Lee Nordness, 1970, was one of the first books to focus exclusively on the work of contemporary American non-production craftsmen. This publication was instrumental to me in bridging the image of the romantic nineteenth-century craftsman and the exciting contemporary object-maker. Becoming a modern artist/craftsman became a real, even practical, objective.

*Golden Flight* by Priscilla Sage, 26" x 46", 1976.

Photo by Kathleen Saccopolous .

Even more influential than people in books and magazines were the real people in my life. I had some wonderful artists and teachers supporting me. I was introduced to fiber artist Priscilla Sage during a visit to her home/studio for a university textile class. Her place was different than the homes I had known. She had polished wood floors, colorful prints by Sister Mary Corita, hand-made ceramics, and one of her wonderful soft sculpture mobiles hung in the stairwell. Her garage was covered with pictures painted by neighborhood kids. It was an inviting atmosphere of comfortable creativity, an environment that I have tried to emulate in my own life.

Priscilla's work was exciting, too. It was graceful, large, dramatic, and made of fiber. I related to her work and the way it was made, and I began to engineer and construct my own three-dimensional shapes with fabric. I made life-size people, shoes,

hamburgers, space costumes with plastic tubing, and fiber optics. I found fabric to be adaptable to any shape and subject. Of course, Claus Oldenberg's giant soft sculptures of everyday objects were very popular then, too.

Another major influence was my future husband, Greg Gantner. Together we encouraged each other to follow the artist's path. We were determined to lead a pure, artistic life at all costs. Our attitude, no doubt, was born under the influence of nineteenth-century romantics with independent incomes. Nonetheless, it has been the underlying philosophy of our life together. This seemed quite reasonable at the time.

Greg and I graduated from Iowa State University without any practical preparations for joining the world. When we moved to Chicago in 1977, all we had was optimism, enthusiasm, talent, and each other. Our creative drive was quite undeniable, so we just followed it. Life was beautiful, but up until now someone else had been paying the bills. Could we maintain our integrity and afford to eat at the same time? Our constant challenge, sometimes a brutal struggle, has been to live up to our own stubborn scale of artistic honesty.

INSP

My first job in the real world was as a sign maker and, eventually, display designer for Crate & Barrel. It was wonderful to be surrounded by yards of colorful, bold Marimekko® fabric and other well-designed objects. But what about my own work? I remained uncommitted to any specific medium, as neither metal nor fabric had captured my devotion. I spent this period consciously searching for my perfect medium. I went to galleries and pored through books and magazines. I wanted to become an expert, a master of a medium that best expressed my ideas, the medium that I could most relate to. But which one?

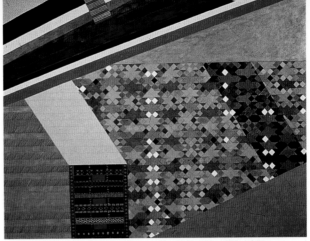

*tent-roof-floor-carpet* by Joyce Kozloff, 96" x 78", 1975.
Photo by eeva-inkeri.

Greg and Jane's Giant Jack-in-the-Box, 3' x 4', 1978. Greg and I were both working at Crate & Barrel. They borrowed our Jack-in-the-Boxes for the windows to advertise a big sale. Greg sculpted the creature and I decorated the box with cut paper designs and made the costume.

At this time, a new art movement was being recognized and praised in important art journals. It was dubbed the Ornamental or Decorative Movement and had evolved from feminist art. Women artists were using everyday household objects to make political statements. People were incorporating aprons, table linens, lace, and other "feminine" objects in their compositions. Their artwork also began to include geometric and floral decorative patterns, since the woman is traditionally the "decorator" in our society. Eventually, these intense ornamental surfaces became the dominant motif of the work. Miriam Schapiro made canvases shaped like giant fans and huge kimonos collaged with a rich mixture of paint and fabric. Joyce Kozloff filled her surfaces with colorful and intense geometric patterns.

IRATION

This interest in ornament was not limited to women. Lucus Summaras was making stunning collages with torn fabric strips and Robert Zakanitch created paintings of luxurious floral repeat patterns.

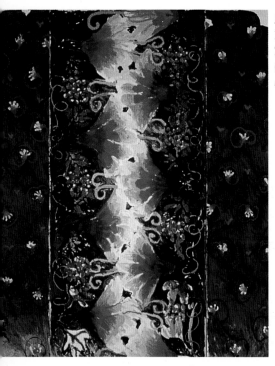

*Flash* by Robert Rahway Zakanitch, 60" x 80", 1978.

*Photo by Robert Rahway Zakanitch.*

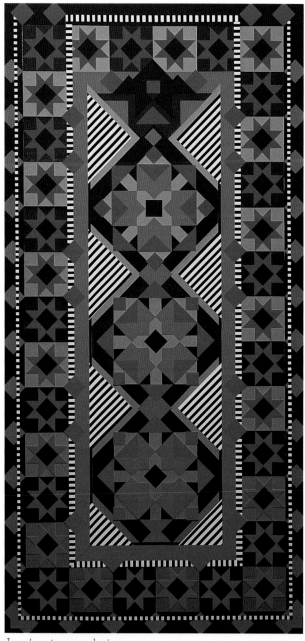

Jane's cut paper design

Simultaneously, I had been making sheets of pattern, often quilt-like, from precisely cut colored papers. I loved making them, but couldn't justify their existence until these other works began to appear. Then I knew that I was part of a contemporary phenomenon, the renewed interest in pattern and design. My subconscious had been caught on a wave of new thought. Even though no one knew my work existed, I began to give myself more credit. I plunged into designing pattern and ornament with enthusiasm and a clear conscience.

▲ *March Study* by Nancy Crow, 80" x 80", 1979.
Hand quilted by Mrs. Levi Mast.

Photo by Mellisa Karlin Mahoney, courtesy of Quilter's Newletter Magazine.

Although many of my cut paper designs incorporated quilt-like patterns, it didn't occur to me to translate these designs into fabric until I saw Nancy Crow's quilt on the cover of *American Craft* magazine in 1980. It was like a pie in the face! Of course! Quilting was the perfect medium! Quilting combined all the elements I desired. It was fabric, a medium that I loved and was already familiar with. It was graphic and colorful, oversized and dramatic. Quilts required craftsmanship and engineering, but they could be done at home without special equipment and allowed for the independence and flexibility that I desired. There was no doubt in my mind, and from that day on, I have been devoted to art quilts.

Too enthusiastic to wait for instructions, I set off unaided. My first few quilts had ⅝" seams (the standard for dressmaking) instead of ¼" seams. But they looked fine, and I just kept learning by making mistakes. Not surprisingly, my first quilts were strip-pieced and geometric, like Nancy Crow's. They were planned on paper and colored so I knew how each quilt would look before it was made. Over time, however, I have uncovered my individual voice and my work has changed. Today my quilts are organic and appliquéd, and the finished design is not always predetermined. In this book you will follow my personal evolution and learn some of my design and construction techniques that have developed along the way.

▲ *Tracks I*, 50" x 50", 1980, artist's collection.
Jane's first quilt.

Photo by Gregory Gantner.

## CLAIMING YOUR CREATIVITY

I believe our creativity comes from a divine source; it is a gift. We are meant to use these gifts and their use becomes a form of praise. We should accept that this creative impulse is God's own plan; therefore, we are obligated to recognize and nurture our talent. Consequently, I give priority to my imagination even when attending to routine daily chores, and I am quite willing to drop daily maintenance altogether when the muse strikes.

I am only able to pursue these things freely because I claimed my position as an artist from the beginning. Consequently, my family and my work grew up together. Everyone in my home knows I'd rather be designing and making quilts than anything else. This is what I do, and my family knows it. They participate in the creation of each piece as it evolves. They comment and cajole, tease me and praise me. They are my most important audience and toughest critics.

When my children were small, it was the same. I didn't spend a lot of time entertaining them. I began working at home as a freelance designer of decorative accessories (plates, vases, candle holders, etc.) when my first-born was three weeks old. I did my work in the middle of the house with the children's activity all around me, as I still do today. When I wasn't designing decorative accessories, I was working on one of my quilts. I was always there; if they needed me, I was available.

They grew up watching me work and often working alongside me. If I had an assignment designing egg cups or picture frames, then the kids designed them too. I always submitted copies of their work along with my own. My son was three when he received his first payment (two dollars) from a client—true encouragement for a budding artist. Today he has evolved into an artist in his own right.

Oliver drawing on the back porch, 1987

Oliver's drawing for a Shakespeare report, 1999

Willow sewing, age 6, 1990

Willow's beaded bag, 1998

My daughter, too, just assumed that her mother was permanently at work. One morning as she played on the floor around my work table, she said, "Mommy, let's pretend that we're at the park. But don't worry, there's a sewing machine there." I must admit, I was rather horrified at her observation, but she said it with total acceptance and she was simply incorporating me into her play. Today she can whip up any three-dimensional fiber object and has an extreme amount of patience for detailed handwork.

My husband is a major contributor to our creative environment. His collection of bizarre and interesting found objects and sculptures are sprinkled throughout the house. Our home has always been like a workshop and museum: often cluttered and confusing, but always productive. Some people would call this devotion to work obsessive, but I believe it has been unavoidable. My husband and I were both born with an innate drive to be independent and creative; consequently, we have to put up with each other.

Not everyone is given such a dose of persistence and determination or a husband with common interests. There are scores of women in my classes who are struggling to reclaim their creative lives. Some of them have set aside their other selves for so long that they actually fear their families will fall apart or their husbands will stop loving them if they begin taking the time for the things they really enjoy. Perhaps they will, perhaps not.

It is never too late to rekindle an old goal or acquire a new attitude. Of course, families need to be taken care of, and we all run into occasional potholes of doubt and discouragement. However, if your determination is strong enough, and you claim your creativity loud enough, the two activities can exist together successfully.

If you need more encouragement to "follow your bliss," there are many books and publications available today about creative people and the creative process. One of my favorite books is *Dawns and Dusks*, an interview with American sculptress Louise Nevelson, another powerful mentor who has fed me and confirmed my purpose in life again and again. She was outspoken, determined, exciting, and eccentric. She didn't achieve recognition until later in life, but she was no less convinced of her talent when she was unrecognized.

## MAINTAINING A
## CREATIVE ENVIRONMENT

One of the most important ways of maintaining the muse is by allowing yourself to live in an environment (both mentally and physically) that promotes excitement, interest, and most of all, productivity. By this I don't mean having the perfect environment. Very few of us have the resources to possess the perfect home and studio. However, it is a true measure of your desire to make the most out of what you have. You must be willing to do the best with the cards you've been dealt and not keep waiting for that golden day when everything is ideal, as it may never come.

When people see my output of quilts over the years they usually assume that I must have a great studio and working environment. Ha! If they only knew! I am a master of "making do" because my desire to work is too strong to be denied.

I work on a small table in the middle of the house, in what is supposed to be the dining room. There are no doors and there is no privacy. My world revolves around that table. You must pass my station to get anywhere in our home. The sewing machine is always there and is only put away for a few days around Christmas, when it's impossible to accomplish anything anyway.

Even though my work area is far less than an ideal studio, it has turned out to be the perfect solution for combining parenthood and livelihood. I haven't missed any of the children's minor daily or major life events, and they have accompanied me on my journey, too. Even now, when I consider a studio in a separate space, I hesitate, because I feel that part of the kids' education will be taken away from them. The workshop and museum atmosphere in our house has influenced so much of who they are.

My husband is equally influential in creating the atmosphere in our home. Greg is a filmmaker and sculptor. He is dangerously creative, very intuitive, and somewhat of an outsider artist. A collector and collager of found objects, he has an uncanny nose for finding things that have been run over by big trucks—several times. Between my fabric and his stuff, an interesting environment is inevitable.

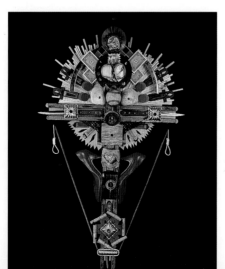

*Crucifix II* by Gregory Gantner, a found objects sculpture, ©1998, private collection.

*Photo by Gregory Gantner.*

A very small part of our book collection

Book collecting is another shared passion in our home. A beautiful book cannot fail to buoy your spirit. Even the knowledge that a book simply sits on your shelf patiently anticipating your touch adds strength to your creative support system.

# FABRIC COLLECTION

Everyone has their own intimate relationship with fabric. We are tightly wrapped in soft, warm blankets when we are born and, from that point on, we are in constant physical contact with fabric until the shroud covers us after death. It not only protects us from heat and cold but also soothes or irritates us. Special fabrics decorate the important ceremonies of our lives. The fabrics we wear and surround ourselves with also express our personalities and can even identify us in our society.

Watch people browse through a fabric or clothing store. They cruise the aisles, running their hands along the tops of the bolts or feeling the random sleeve. Fabric evokes a sensual response. The color, texture, and feel of fabric can trigger memories and promote dreams of a glamorous future.

Quilters are especially sensitive to fabric. Most of us have such strong connections with fabric that often we can't bear to leave the store without at least a small piece of that delicious yardage in our possession. There are many notorious cases of fabric addiction in the quilt world. I once had a student who claimed that she had to build a new home just so she could contain her bounteous collection of fabric. What a thrilling thought!

Most quilters have been collecting fabric for years and have compiled an incredible stockpile to select from when designing pieces. Like books, our cloth sits on the shelf laden with creative potential, waiting to be of service.

My fabric collection is relatively meager for twenty years of quilting. Being an artist of modest means and limited space has made me very frugal when making textile purchases. I do a lot of scrounging around the bargain tables and am able to resist almost all impulse buying. This is possible because I use mostly solid-colored cottons, not fashionable or seasonal prints. The prints I use in my work are usually simple geometrics, such as stripes, polka dots, checks, and plaids. I want the fabric to become my own creation, and this is difficult if the fabric is already a work of art in itself. I may use a fancy designer fabric for making summer dresses or window curtains, but not for my quilts. I also prefer to avoid the fashions and trends of quilting so that my work remains personal. I am not against using designer prints, since some of them are quite stunning; they are simply not appropriate for my work.

I also buy large pieces of fabric, usually at least two yards. When I find a good color or pattern, I use it again and again. For example, if you study

My 8' x 9½' office is the same tiny room that holds my fabric collection. The walls are lined with insulation board and covered with paper so I am surrounded with inspiration.

my quilts, you will find an orange-dotted Swiss, certain black-and-white plaids, and a green fabric with little dots in a half-dozen designs.

Once the fabrics are home, they are washed then arranged in stacks by color. There is enough to choose from at this point to find any color I might need.

## SEWING MACHINES

I recommend that new quilt enthusiasts keep their sewing machine visible and accessible at all times. Let your family get used to it. Believe it or not, there really isn't a law that jails people who don't put away their sewing machine every night. However, it is the most convenient and frequently-used excuse for not accomplishing any real work. If you're determined to succeed, you will find a way to make work happen. By letting the world see your sewing machine, you are making the declaration, "This is what I do! Like it or lump it!"

I also encourage you to surround your work area with inspiring objects and pictures. Make your space a home for your muse, a place to dream and scheme. The more personal you can make your space, the more inviting and the easier to work in it will be.

## THE BENEFITS OF DAYDREAMING

I have always been a daydreamer. As a child, it interfered with learning, but as I got older, day-dreams became projections of the future—a space where all things became possible. I could see life before me and act as if that future was a reality.

Today, this natural ability for the imagination to sustain a mental picture is called creative visualiza-tion. We all use creative visualization, usually sub-consciously. We use it to our detriment as well as to our benefit. If we worry, we are visualizing disaster. If we hope, we are visualizing success. Obviously, both ways of thinking have the power to affect your attitude and your actions. If we can learn to direct our visions, we can break down some of the internal barriers that keep us from our full potential.

I actually recommend daydreaming as a potent tool for enhancing your life. Over the years, I have tapped my daydreams to summon my muse. I have developed a ritual to trigger my receptivity to creative possibilities.

I begin most mornings by looking at beautiful pictures. The colors, shapes, or atmosphere of a picture catch my imagination and set my dream-ing-self free to wander. Once my imagination has been sparked, I let it ascend to the primary operat-ing position for a day of creative work. At this point, I can actually feel waves of well-being and the tingle of unknown possibilities rising through my body. The mood of anticipation has been established and, if all goes well, this receptivity and heightened awareness will open the mental flood gates and manifest itself in some interesting work.

Many creative people have a system to kick-start their imaginations. For some, it's music that gets ideas flowing, or a strict daily routine, or going for a walk. There are as many ways to court the muse as there are artists. As you work and dream, listen to your senses to discover where your muse lives. Once you find her hiding places, it will be easier to call on her on a regular schedule.

# THE GARDEN

Thanks to his Greg's nurturing, our backyard is a magical hideaway from the hassles of city life. Here in our private little garden, we are enveloped with layers of protective greenery.

Greg's garden is dense with drama. The flowers he plants are theatrical and have definite attitudes. They are often oversized, fluorescent, spikey or curly, even poisonous. Every year there are several varieties of angel's trumpets, also called thorn apple or jimsonweed. Their huge white trumpet blossoms open in the evening, releasing a lovely scent. You can sit in a chair and actually watch the long buds unwind.

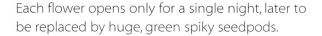

Each flower opens only for a single night, later to be replaced by huge, green spiky seedpods.

We also have a purple variety of angel's trumpet. They have deep, double purple trumpets with white lining and shiny black-purple stems. They look quite decadent and mysterious.

Every year, sunflowers and pumpkins sneak their way into the garden, thanks to the squirrels. Greg builds trellises and bridges of sticks and twine to train the pumpkins up to the garage roof, where they will get lots of sun and have a dry surface to grow on. Deep purple morning glories create a "living wall" on one fence, and hibiscus line the other. A blue spruce takes up a generous portion of the yard, but it is hollowed out underneath to create a secret playroom.

Greg also enjoys making yard art, and part of each weekend is usually spent creating vignettes and building outdoor sculptures with found objects. Bowling balls, billiard balls, and mirror balls are scattered here and there. Temporary environmental sculptures of petals, leaves, sticks, rocks, earth, and snow transform the yard into a seasonal museum.

This joyous living energy feeds me enough inspirational material to last through the long, gray Chicago winters— what better time to quilt and dream about the garden?

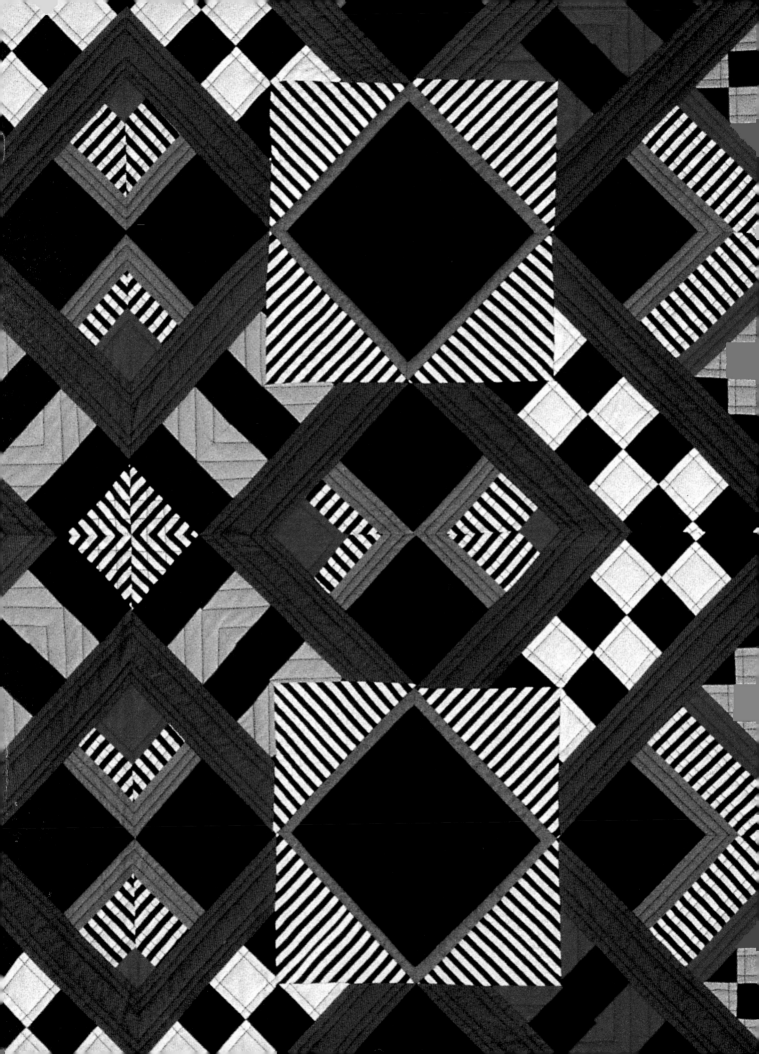

# the quilts
## 1980-1999

## THE FIRST QUILTS

As I have mentioned, seeing Nancy Crow's quilt *March Study* on the cover of *American Craft* magazine was a major influence on my decision to become an art quilter. Consequently, my first quilts were also composed of strip-piecing and were very geometric. Blissfully ignorant of the rules of quilt construction, I was able to ignore standard block construction.

▲ *Tracks*, 65" x 65", ©1985, private collection.

*Photo by Gregory Gantner.*

Tracks was one of my earliest pieces. I started it in 1981, around the time my first child was born. As many of you know, giving birth is wonderfully inspirational, but you are unable to do a thing with that inspiration. So this quilt remained an unquilted top for many frustrating years. I finally got so discouraged that I quilted it by machine (not an acceptable solution back then). Machine quilting was the best remedy for me, because even though I enjoyed hand quilting, I had too many design ideas to spend a year quilting each piece.

▲ *Summertime (Cinderella Quilt)*, 78" x 78"
©1981-1986, artist's collection.

*Photo by Gregory Gantner.*

*Summertime* is very important in my evolution as an artist. I also call it my Cinderella quilt. This quilt sat in a quilting frame for almost four years, from the time my son was a toddler until my daughter (three years younger) was a toddler. I worked on it when I could, between freelance work and making lunches for messy kids in highchairs. I was proud of this quilt and knew it was good.

I watched the art quilt movement grow, seemingly without me. Penny McMorris hosted a wonderful quilt show on PBS that kept my goal to be an art quilter alive. I also started attending the Illinois Quilter's Guild monthly meetings, quietly sitting in the back row and absorbing everything. I was frustrated because I knew what I was creating in my isolated little corner, though no one else seemed to.

To make things worse, at every guild meeting, a small, attractive red-haired woman got up for show-and-tell. She would hold up a fabulous quilt and recite the prizes it had just won or the show it was about to be in. I came home after every meeting green with envy and overflowing with sour grapes. I complained to my husband, "That woman was there again!" She made me angry because she was doing exactly what I wanted to do, but nobody even knew I existed. There sat my quilt in its frame, beautiful and unfinished. You may have guessed that this unsuspecting thorn-in-my-side was Caryl Bryer Fallert. Caryl's success motivated me into action and made me realize the power of my determination.

When *Summertime* was finally finished, I took it to the guild meeting. Even though I was deathly afraid of public speaking, I stood in line for show and tell. My knees were shaking and my heart was pounding so loud that I was sure the entire room could hear it. The Illinois Quilter's Guild is large, so when our work was held up we had to go onto a stage and speak into a microphone. It was probably the most difficult thing I've ever done. I don't know what I said, I was actually quivering with fright. But when they held up my quilt, the entire room gave a loud gasp. They seemed to be surprised and delighted. It was the first public recognition of my very quiet quilting career. I went back to my chair, glowing red with embarrassment, so horrified and happy it was over that I could have wept.

When the meeting was finished, Caryl was instantly at my side, inviting me to join a newly formed fiber art critique group called FACET. It was like a dream. I was nobody when I walked in, and by the time I left, my career had finally begun. My work was out of the closet and into the world. That's why I call this piece my Cinderella quilt.

I will be forever grateful to Caryl for innocently irritating me into motion and for being the person who caught me when I finally jumped. She has continued to be a guide to me and many others with her generosity and pioneering spirit. I am thankful, too, for the friendship of all the FACET members. They have supplied a haven of support for many years.

Even though my knowledge of quilt construction was limited to strip-piecing and geometric composition, I knew I wanted my work to express movement and energy. I began to experiment with straight lines and motion by using a process of cutting and pasting with paper.

First, pages of appealing geometric patterns, such as stripes, checks, and triangles, were drawn and liberally machine copied. Then, by cutting and combining different patterns, several interesting new arrangements emerged. These new compositions were copied, cut-up, and reworked. For *Tracks* and *Summertime*, I simply took one of these hybrid designs and repeated it as a mirror image into four, giant reverse right-angle blocks.

*Sun Spiral, Blue Spiral,*
and *Spring Spiral,*
50" x 50" each, ©1987,
corporate collection.

*Photos by Gregory Gantner.*

For this spiral series, the design is repeated in eight triangular wedges without being reversed at all, giving the effect of a fan of cards, each radiating from the center and exposing the same decorated corner of the card. All three quilts were made with the same pattern and are totally strip-pieced. Each pattern piece is cut from a different sheet of pre-pieced fabric. Different combinations of color and patterns (stripes and chevrons) make the attitude of each quilt unique.

# WIGGLY LINES

By simply replacing a straight line with a wavy line my work took on a unique appearance. Rather than looking like the quilts that had initially inspired me, my work began to have a flavor of its own.

◄ *Zig Zag Spiral*, 50" x 50", ©1988, private collection.

*Photo by Gregory Gantner.*

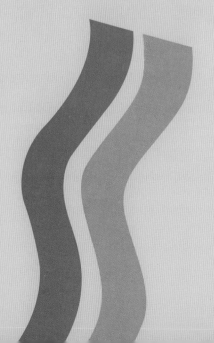

Z*ig Zag Spiral* is also an important quilt. It was my first private commission and the first quilt to have wiggly lines. The design was inspired by some hardy Midwestern thunderstorms. It was first composed on paper, as the previous quilts had been. Again, the action lines of the piece are set on diagonal to accentuate the impression of movement. It has the feeling of a turning spiral or spinning pinwheel, which is an appropriate translation of a whopping spring thunderstorm. The wiggly lines were a gift from the gods and mark the beginning of new design possibilities. They were hand appliquéd and took weeks to attach, but I loved the extra energy they added to the piece.

▲ *Garden Spiral*, 50" x 50" ©1988, artist's collection.

*Photo by Judy Smith-Kressley.*

Garden Spiral continues with the wavy motif. These appliqués took the whole steaming month of August to complete. Again, they looked great, but I knew there had to be a more efficient way to work. I had to line each wave with interfacing so the black background fabric wouldn't shadow through and dull the bright yellow fabric. Thus, from necessity, my current appliqué technique evolved and was put to use on my next quilt.

# APPLIQUÉ AND DIVINE RADIATION

You will notice a change in my work as appliqué and the ability to incorporate curved shapes was realized. Instead of implying the movement of a spiral, I could actually make a spiral shape. Because these shapes are applied to the surface of the quilt and are no longer a structural element but rather a decorative object, I was able to expand my ideas, both emotionally and physically. No longer confined by geometry, I was released into the world of all possibilities.

▲*Divine Radiation*, 69" x 63",
©1989, artist's collection.

*Photo by Judy Smith-Kressley.*

Divine Radiation is a symbolic expression of this expansion. It celebrates new potential and radiates with optimism. This quilt also begins to explore the relationship between the soul, the earth, and the heavens, what I call the "big picture." I believe that my new way of working opened my mind enough to be able to see the "big picture" at last. Spiritual exploration continues to be the underlying theme of all my work.

*Summer Garden*, 69" x 55",
©1989, private collection.

Photo by Judy Smith-Kressley.

**S**ummer Garden was inspired by the flowers that grow in our small yard in a northside neighborhood of Chicago. It is surprising how much vegetation can be squeezed into a tiny space. Every year, we have the most prolific (and eccentric) yard in the neighborhood. My husband plants flowers with the most graphic and exaggerated designs and strong bright colors: orange, red, yellow, purple, and white. I have a particular fondness for flowers with the dramatic combination of red and yellow, such as marigolds, lilies, and gaillardia. The freckles and frilled edges of lilies are endlessly inspiring. All these exciting elements were simply magnified and stylized to become *Summer Garden*.

Some black and white TV test patterns that my husband brought home from work inspired *Information Radiation*. They were the kind of designs that used to be on the black and white TV screen early in the morning, before "Howdy Doody" came on, or after the "Tonight Show," when programming was over for the day. These patterns made me think about the over-whelming abundance of information in our lives.

We are constantly forced to separate the inane from the essential, a skill that is becoming a lost art. Everyone with a television is subjected to the same messages and images and being sold the same products. This quilt refers to the deceptive glamour of mass media as it permeates society with a blanket of mediocrity and sparkling irrele-vance, dulling our consciousness and undermin-ing the individual.

▲*Information Radiation*, 65" x 65", ©1989, artist's collection.

*Photo by Judy Smith-Kressley.*

▲*Light Study*, 36" x 36",
©1989, private collection.

Photo by Gregory Gantner.

**L**ight Study and *Dark Study* are made from the same pattern, but one is done with a dark background and the other with a light one. This simple variation creates an interesting contrast in attitudes as well as color. The spiral, the wavy line, and the spikes are established as part of my design language and are seen in many reincarnations to this day. All of the stripes and gold polka dots in *Dark Study* were hand painted.

▲*Dark Study*, 36" x 36",
©1989, private collection.

Photo by Gregory Gantner.

▲*Waves*, 60" x 58",
©1990, artist's collection.

*Photo by Judy Smith-Kressley.*

**W**aves is unique to my designs, because it uses a repeated block; however, the block is askew instead of square. The colors within the spirals gradually change as they move across the surface.

▲*Night Garden*, 61" x 63",
©1991, private collection.

Photo by Gregory Gantner.

Night Garden is another piece that floated into my consciousness almost full-grown. In hindsight, I see the influence of Japanese kimonos, Art Nouveau, and Art Deco filtering through the composition. The central panel of graduating circles looks like light reflected on a pond or fireflies strobing on a summer night. The bordering panels resemble reeds and grasses on water's edge. As often happens, quilts reveal their symbols and sources only after they are made.

This quilt is also notable because of the intense labor it demanded. Although a circle is a simple graphic element, making a circle in fabric requires patience and precision. To machine appliqué a circle, the entire body of the quilt must be turned and guided through the small sewing machine armhole several times simply to attach the appliqué. Furthermore, because each circle is also echo quilted over the entire black background, this quilt was slowly revolving through the machine for days. The process was so intense, that now I think long and hard for alternative possibilities to creating a simple circle.

*Night Sky*, 20" x 23",
©1993, private collection.

Night Sky and Night Garden II are variations of the larger *Night Garden* piece. Simple, sparse, and graphic, they condense and focus the elements of earth, sky, and water, much like a close-up photograph. Here again, the influence of Japanese kimonos and turn-of-the-century European design is evident.

*Night Garden II*, 24" x 24",
©1990, private collection.

As my quilts began to take on more symbolism, I started to connect with the work of other artists who were also concerned with the relationship between earthly life, the soul, and the heavens. Much of the art of Western civilization was commissioned for religious institutions, so there is plenty to explore. I found myself especially drawn to the atmospheric fourteenth-century altar pieces of Jan van Eyck and Rogier van der Weyden. These altar pieces were often painted with three or more connecting panels, often long and thin, called polyptychs, which depict the three levels on which life was thought to be experienced: heaven, earth, and hell. *Eden* represents the earthly and heavenly plains in a similar format. The flower shape at the bottom of the quilt symbolizes earth, and the wings near the top, heaven.

*Heaven's Gift*, 78" x 60",
©1990, collection of Mary Lou Haines.

*Photo by Judy Smith-Kressley.*

In 1990, my friend and favorite art director died of AIDS. We had worked together for many years. His memorial service was in an art gallery in downtown Chicago. Arranged throughout the rooms were his most spectacular designs—five-foot candelabras and giant colored glass vases. I thought how wonderful it was to have these objects remaining as symbols of his creativity and markers of his life.

As I pondered the relationship between work and life, I suddenly realized that we are obligated to use our given talents. We are given special abilities to advance our civilization and the evolution of our souls. By embracing our talents, we not only fulfill our purpose on earth, but also glorify the giver. *Heaven's Gift* symbolizes the joyous exchange of gifts between heaven and earth.

E very year my husband plants sunflowers. We let them prosper wherever they happen to sprout, often in unexpected places. The power of sunflowers is irresistible. They are the peasants of the garden—noble, naïve, and stubbornly hearty, innocent and magnificent. Very few artists seem to be able to resist their magnetism. The sunflowers in my quilts have been severely stylized into simple circles, radiating their timeless attraction.

▲ *Sun Flowers*, 24" x 42", ©1992, private collection.

*Photo by Judy Smith-Kressley.*

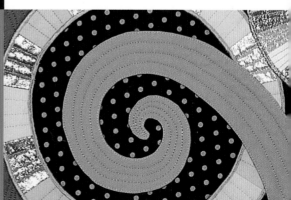

*S*un Day is a simple celebration of life. This theme is at the center of all my work: the magnificence of creation and the flowering of a soul. Here the sun radiates as the imaginary plants uncurl and gravitate to its life-giving power. The background is made by strip-piecing fabrics of gradually changing colors. The sun is repeated in the side panels above a wave-like spiral of blues and greens.

▲ *Sun Day*, 71" x 52",
©1992, artist's collection.

*Photo by Judy Smith-Kressley.*

▲ *Spring Garden*, 54½" x 56",
©1992, artist's collection.

*Photo by Judy Smith-Kressley.*

Spring Garden was inspired by a wonderful spring in Chicago. Almost every little yard has a rose bush or trellis in our city neighborhood, but this particular year the roses were extraordinary. Even tiny urban plots of earth can hold many wonders. I am constantly amazed and inspired. Like my mother once said, "It sure doesn't take much to make you happy!"

As wavy lines kept invading my work, I became increasingly aware of their symbolism to me. These lines became the connecting web between the ethereal and the physical body. They symbolized the radiation of the sun, of the soul, and of the spirit, all originating from a central source and reaching outward.

In *Heaven and Earth*, wavy lines radiate from heaven and penetrate earth. Heaven is a traditional and idealized representation, all-powerful and perfect. Here, heaven radiates like the sun over the thriving green planet, which seems to be self-sufficient and oblivious to the invisible and immeasurable influence of the spiritual light.

▲ *Heaven and Earth*, 64" x 64", ©1992, private collection.

*Photo by Gregory Gantner.*

**T**rouble in the Garden represents our earth and our lives in a society obsessed with consumption. Material possessions have become so important that many are willing to give up their freedom to acquire them. A society is in trouble when greed is the main lesson learned in school. This quilt suggests the inevitable eruption when people and the planet rebel against the warped values that restrict and corrode the quality of their lives and environment. We really do live in the Garden of Eden. When the big storm hits, it will be ugly and painful, but it may be necessary for cleansing and healing. It is housekeeping in the Garden of Eden.

Technically, *Trouble in the Garden* was an interesting challenge. Each shape was made individually. The leaves, spirals, clouds, and lightning are separate pieces that were arranged and rearranged until I liked the composition. The leaves are made of two layers of fabric adhered together with fusible web. I cut out the vein from the center of the top layer so that the bottom darker fabric would show through. Then, I carefully attached one shape to another until the whole top was constructed. This process left me with a stack of leftover vein shapes. I ended up liking the shape so much that now I make them deliberately.

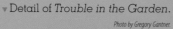
▾ Detail of *Trouble in the Garden*.
*Photo by Gregory Gantner.*

▴ *Collage*, 29" x 46",
©1994, artist's collection.
*Photo by Gregory Gantner.*

**C**ollage is made entirely of leftover and trimmed-away pieces from previous work. The predetermined shapes and colors had a life of their own and dictated the composition. If you study this quilt, you'll find where some of the shapes originated. (Hint: Look at *Trouble in the Garden*.)

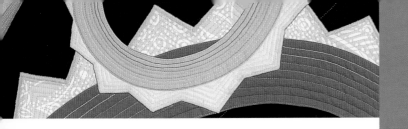

# THE TREE OF LIFE

The deeper I get into my own fiber art, the more interested I have become in the needlework of the past. The quiet intensity of this intimate discipline with needle and thread has existed for centuries. Ancient embroiderers were doing more than just ornamenting textiles; they were stitching protective powers into fiber with symbolic patterns based on their mythology and superstition.

The Tree of Life is one of the most common symbols to be found in embroidery and fiber art around the world. The tree represents fertility, birth, maturity, death, and rebirth—all the cycles of life, for both trees and humans. A tree is also a link between the three planes of life. Its roots are in the underworld and its head is in the heavens, while the trunk bridges those two worlds. In Christian art, the tree also represents the Tree of Knowledge, the apple-bearing tree that overwhelmed Adam and Eve in the Garden of Eden.

Personally, the needlework tree is also a symbolic web between ancient artisans and contemporary fiber artists, not only a continuation of the desire to express ourselves with needle and thread, but also a willingness to give ourselves over to the solitary contemplation and repetitive actions required to produce our work. We are joined by a mysterious determination and an ability to concentrate beyond the boundaries of many other humans on earth.

I also believe that my work is embodied with "magical" powers, just as the ancient artisans believed. Each quilt has been created with intense concentration and conscious attention to detail. They demand my attention until they have absorbed enough energy to stand on their own in the world. In using the tree motif, it is my desire to join head, heart, and hands with an ancient tradition to protect and encourage the world with needle and thread.

Spring is the season that influences my work the most. I receive enough inspiration each spring to last through winter. It is thrilling to watch new life unfurl from the dark earth and to see the planet's unstoppable life-force reawakened. The fresh green sprouts of daylilies are always among the first to appear in Chicago gardens. These tiny adventurers with their bright opposing leaves inspired the exuberant tree motif in *Tree of Life: Spring*. My love of folk art influenced this piece as well. Purple, yellow, and green seem to be the perfect colors for new life and its creative energy and just the palette for a quilt about hope, growth, and renewal.

The elements on *Tree of Life: Spring* are all appliquéd to a whole cloth background. The tree was put together as one big unit, then attached to the background so I could cut away the black fabric underneath to let the colors be as bright as possible. This quilt was so labor intensive that I almost swore off quilting forever. Of course, I create my own headaches because of the fastidious way that I work. When it was finished, I devoted the next year to making smaller, more manageable quilts and replenishing my energy.

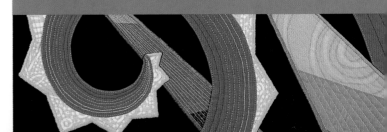

▲ *Tree of Life: Spring*, 70" x 80",
©1994, artist's collection.

*Photo by Judy Smith-Kressley.*

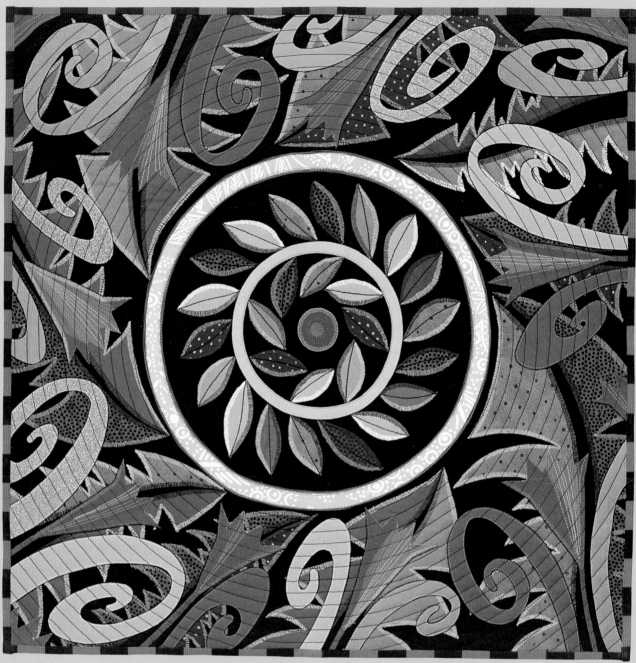

▲ *Wreath*, 22" x 22",
©1996, artist's collection.

*Photo by Gregory Gantner.*

**W**reath was designed to represent the letter "O" in a show of alphabet quilts. I chose the letter "O" because my son's name is Oliver and we sometimes use "O" as his nickname. Since the circular wreath is a traditional quilt motif, I thought it would be appropriate to use here. Leaning weeds and flowers surround the wreath, accentuating the circular movement.

*O*vergrown Garden attempts to capture the inexhaustible vitality of nature. This garden is organized but has become a gloriously undisciplined field of energy. Each flower contributes its glory to the overall radiant effect. We are all flowers in the garden.

▲ *Overgrown Garden,* 27½" x 41", ©1994, artist's collection.

*Photo by Gregory Gantner.*

▲ *Memory Garden,* 25½" x 37", ©1995, private collection.

*Photo by Judy Smith-Kressley.*

*M*emory Garden is composed of leftover shapes from previous quilts. It also includes two small pieces of old print fabric that a friend found while renovating a house. They are on the upper left and lower right sides of the composition. Like a traditional quilt made of clothing scraps, this quilt kept the memory of where it had been before.

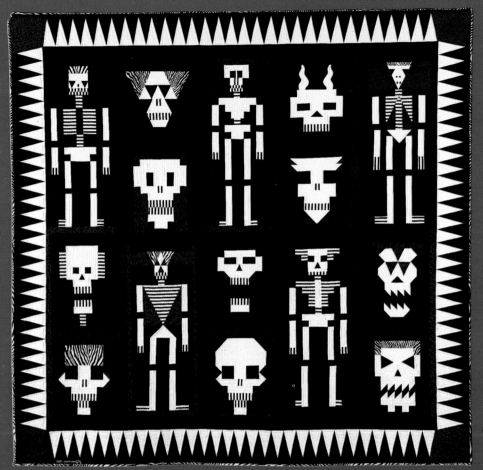

◀ *Skeleton Quilt I*, 72" x 69",
©1988, artists collection.

Skeletons have always fascinated my husband and me. They are wonderful reminders of our mortality, as well as a great graphic design—a perfect subject for the high-contrast designs I'm attracted to. Shown here are two quilts that were made strictly for fun. One of them hangs in our living room during the month of October, but it has been know to still be on display during the Christmas season. The other quilt hangs in a corporate accounting office. I like to imagine that it is keeping the employees honest.

▲ *Skeleton Quilt II*, 63" x 63",
©1988, corporate collection.

▲ *Day of the Dead,* 22½" x 21½",
©1996, artist's collection.

*Photo by Judy Smith-Kressley.*

**D**ay of the Dead was made for an invitational quilt show called Calendar Girls. Each artist was to make a small quilt about a holiday. I claimed November 1st and 2nd—All Saints Day and All Souls Day in Mexico. This celebration has always fascinated me. The Mexican culture isn't afraid to acknowledge the spirit, as anyone who has visited a Mexican church or read Mexican writers knows.

On these holidays, families make shrines for their deceased relatives and ancestors. The shrines are decorated with food, flowers, candles, candies, and toys. Spirits of children visit on November 1st and adult spirits on the 2nd. Families go to the cemetery to give offerings and decorate the graves. The bakeries make special cookies and candies decorated with skulls and crosses and fancy, colorful sugar skulls for this festive occasion. I wanted this quilt to express this colorful celebration of the cycles of life, so I created a skull with worms crawling in and out, surrounded by flowers.

# SILHOUETTE QUILTS—TWO FOR ONE

Around 1995, I began making silhouette quilts. These quilts have a central tree of life silhouette bordered by an intensely patterned frame. The quilt begins as a whole cloth of heavy black cotton duck. Then the tree and its frame are precisely cut out with a very sharp X-Acto® knife. The surrounding negative shape (the square surrounding the tree) is then removed. What still remains of the whole cloth is placed on top of a contrasting background fabric and attached with a matching black satin stitch. The leftover negative piece is placed on its own contrasting whole cloth background. Consequently, I am getting two quilts from every design. Even though the initial design is identical (only reversed in color) the resulting quilts are quite different in mood and message. The following quilts are grouped in pairs; each has the same central tree silhouette, which was cut from the original black whole cloth background.

▲ *Thorn Garden*, 24" x 24", ©1995, private collection.

Photo by Judy Smith-Kressley.

*Thorn Garden* is the first quilt in the silhouette series. The central motif is a stylized tree. The green fabric behind the tree is hand-painted cotton. The green thorns are stenciled with fabric paints and further defined with an outline of white and purple quilting stitches. The fanciful purple spirals are machine appliquéd then finished with additional hand embroidery.

*Tree of Life: Bandana*, 33½" x 33½",
©1995, artist's collection.

After removing the negative background shape (the square surrounding the tree) from *Thorn Garden*, I adhered it to a square of red fabric. There was no reason for choosing red other than liking the color and the black-and-red combination. I hadn't even an inkling of where this piece would lead. As it evolved, it took on the look of a bandana or kerchief. I realized that my work not only was made of fabric, but also was about fabric. I was making textiles about textiles, absorbing centuries of pattern and subconsciously re-creating them. A profusion of growth surrounds this very formal barbed tree.

**M**y mother commissioned *Tree of Life: Summer* for her new home. She picked a stack of fabrics for me to use. Light blue, a color I'd only used as an accent in my previous work, was to be the predominate color. It's difficult for me to be confined to an inflexible palette, but for Mom I toughed it out.

As the quilt evolved on the work wall, the whole family felt obligated to give their opinions. "It's way too wild for Grandma!" and "Mom! That's a hippy quilt!" Well, Mom and Dad have it hanging on their wall, at least when I come to visit. Points of pulsating energy measure the spine of the tree, very much like the chakra centers of the human body (in Kundalini yoga). The tree mirrors our own lives: in this case, a time of fertility, energy, and opulent growth.

▼ Detail of *Tree of Life: Summer*.
*Photo by Judy Smith-Kressley.*

▲ *Tree of Life: Summer*, 24½" x 39½", ©1995, private collection.
*Photo by Judy Smith-Kressley.*

▲ *Resurrection*, 28½" x 42",
©1995, collection of Mary Lou Haines.

*Photo by Judy Smith-Kressley.*

Resurrection is the negative silhouette from *Tree of Life: Summer*, but this quilt turned out to be a stark contrast from its partner. It is desolate and barren; all the leaves have been stripped away and a severe red light radiates on the surface. However, there is an underlying hopefulness. New growth is sprouting from the naked branches and wreathes, and a symbol of renewal decorates the bottom cornes.

As I was looking for inspiration at the library one afternoon, I came across a picture of a wonderful embroidered jacket from the early seventeenth century. It was a delightful combination of elegance and wit. It tickled me so much that I decided to do a quilt with the same feeling. Also, I had recently discovered other historic works of "millefleurs" (many flowers)—paintings, tapestries, and embroideries completely filled with flowers. They have a refreshing quality of innocence and opulence. This was the attitude I wanted to reproduce.

My design was to be built around a willow tree silhouette. Since my daughter's name is Willow, this was an obvious choice. As I worked on this quilt, she was always in my thoughts. This quilt absorbed all my encouragement and hopes for her future.

*Willow* began as a whole black cloth with the tree cut out of the center. After attaching the white fabric behind the tree, the fun of filling in the border began. Once the flowers and butterflies began to appear, they demanded more and more company. The quilt was not happy until every space was filled. I was both delighted and horrified as the wall became saturated with growth. I repositioned the flowers until a sense of order was achieved, and I didn't attach anything permanently until the composition was final. By then, I had several hundred pins impaling the quilt to the wall! The quilt top was immobile until every element was adhered, so starting at the edge, one pin was removed at a time so the nose of the iron could slowly fuse the pieces onto the background. All the ironing happened on the design wall, often with me standing on a ladder.

After each flower, leaf, and bug was tacked on, the intense process of stitching began. This quilt is a labor of love. I gave it intense concentration and attention to every detail. Its message is totally optimistic; I think this is why it has attracted so much attention.

▲ *Brambles, Willow's Weeds,* and *Crown of Thorns,* 24" x 24" each, ©1996, private collection.

Photos by Gregory Gantner.

Brambles, Willow's Weeds, and *Crown of Thorns* were designed as a triptych, three pieces shown together. They each have densely patterned borders around a single tree silhouette. Their gardens are plagued with calamity. Thorns, burrs, and weeds foreshadow imminent danger. The title *Willow's Weeds* is derived from "widow's weeds," the black mourning clothes worn by a widow. *Crown of Thorns* is an obvious reference to Christ's crown, a symbol of struggle and persecution. It is often difficult to cultivate optimism when you must keep defending yourself from the weeds. Life is hard.

This sampler triptych was created with the negative tree silhouettes from *Brambles*, *Willow's Weeds*, and *Crown of Thorns*. Traditionally, samplers were done by young girls to practice and perfect their needlework skills. Girls filled their samplers with alphabets, sentimental verses, and stylized flowers. Of course, much can be said about the social and political constraints that kept women tied to quiet domestic activities such as sewing, but the fact remains that we can see into those young women's lives through these early stitching exercises.

Many years ago, I attended an exhibit of "insane" art. The displayed work was from a turn-of-the-century asylum that allowed the patients to continue practicing their trades. The printers still worked at the press and the carpenters continued to build, only the things they were making were out of the ordinary. In fact, they were absolutely extraordinary. The most powerful piece in the entire exhibit was a woman's jacket that was blue and quite small. Its style was common for its time, short and fitted. What made it exceptional were the rows of embroidered writing that wrapped around the entire jacket from top to bottom. The words were stitched with manic intensity in a heavy black thread. Even though I couldn't read the writing, it left an unforgettable impression of passion and frustration. It was one of the most disturbing things I have ever seen.

As I was making these small quilts, I imagined a happy little girl dutifully stitching on her sampler, unaware of the dramatic events that lay in her future. I wanted my samplers to have an undercurrent of melancholy and potential dementia. Will she be able to hold herself together, or will she be overwhelmed by circumstances like the woman with the jacket?

*Sampler: Leaves,*
*Sampler: Thorn,*
*Sampler: Willow,*
*16½" x 16½" each,*
*©1996, private collection.*

Photos by Gregory Gantner.

▲ *Color Garden*, 43" x 43",
©1994, private collection.

*Photo by Gregory Gantner.*

A garden's character is determined by its combination of plants—its unique mixture of color, textures, and shapes. *Color Garden* is an intuitive tangle of organic shapes orphaned from other quilts. The character of the garden began to emerge as I played with my bags of scraps. This collage technique enables me to work more spontaneously and the results are often delightfully surprising.

▲ *Gloriosa,* 29" x 24",
©1997, private collection.

Lilies, I love them, as these three quilts attest. Their wavy-edged, curly petals and fabulous color combinations leave me breathless. They are obvious subjects for a quilt—a simple celebration of Mother Nature's outrageous creativity.

▼ *Wild Flower,* 24" x 24",
©1997, private collection.

▲ *Visitation*, 50" x 42",
©1997, private collection.

*Photo by Judy Smith-Kressley.*

I made *Visitation* for the Up in the Air show, commemorating the fiftieth anniversary of the UFO sightings in Roswell, New Mexico. Personally, I think that if a soul is evolved enough to visit other planets, it wouldn't need a spaceship. However, I do think that souls visit from other places in other ways. I believe in reincarnation and that there are many levels for souls to experience. Souls from different places and evolutions experience one another often and in a variety of ways.

Since I don't "do" spaceships, it was a challenge to illustrate the UFO theme. I decided to use "The Invasion of the Body Snatchers" concept instead. Remember the movie with the huge unearthly pods growing in everyone's basement, which eventually blossomed into replicas of the people whose homes they inhabited? In *Visitation*, alien vines are reaching and twisting, empowered by the radiation of their home planet.

As often happens, our work reveals our subconscious thoughts, too. It was spring, and as I worked, this piece became rather Easter-like in its symbolism. Unexpectedly, it formed a cross. What better example of a highly evolved soul touching down on our planet? His visit was brief and mysterious. He tried to tip us off to the "big picture" and was defeated by the lower vibrations, only to rise above this earthly existence.

Flower Field is an attempt to capture the energy and random composition of a field or garden. Groupings of color and overlapping shapes create the personality of each field. The dancing red trumpet flower was influenced by a spectacular amaryllis that was blooming in our home that winter.

This quilt is a collage of a few simple shapes: three sizes of flowers, spirals, and trumpet blossoms. Arranging and rearranging the elements can be both fun and frustrating, but you must keep experimenting and adjusting until the composition sings.

*C*rystal Garden is another small quilt
assembled from my collection of
orphaned shapes. It was a snowy
Sunday afternoon and I had an itch to make something. Unwittingly, the fabric selections reflected
the colors and feelings of that cold, gray winter day.

▲ *Crystal Garden*, 24" x 24",
©1998, private collection.

*Photo by Gregory Gantner.*

▲ *Thorn Apple*, 30" x 30",
©1998, artist's collection.

*Photo by Gregory Gantner.*

Each year we grow several varieties of angel's trumpet, also called jimsonweed or thorn apple. They are a relative of deadly nightshade, a poisonous and incredibly dramatic flower. They have huge, pure white sweet smelling trumpet blossoms; large, dusty gray-green leaves; and wonderfully evil-looking spikey seed balls the size of Christmas tree ornaments.

I focused on the leaves and seeds by stylizing and magnifying them dramatically. First, I made a stack of whole leaves and whole seeds and began to play with their arrangement. I like to let the elements continue out of the frame, as in a close-up photograph; your mind completes the picture. You somehow know that this is just a slice of the whole scene and there is more activity on all sides. Next, I trimmed the premade shapes with a rotary cutter. The leftover leaf and seed pieces are always saved for future designs.

S*eeds and Blossoms* is another quilt inspired by angel's trumpets, this time focusing on the huge trumpet blossoms that unwind from cigar-shaped buds with a small curly spiral on their tips. The frame captures a close-up view of vibrating growth and movement. The gray background fabric is stenciled with an all-over leaf pattern. Many of the black dots in the center of the flowers are also painted on.

Almost every spiral I see is profound, but when I saw massive tangles of aloe vera plants on the California coastline I was overwhelmed. Both spirals and spikes! What more could you ask for? I created these pieces as soon as I got back to the studio.

▲ *Curl II*, 16" x 16",
©1999, artist's collection.

Photo by Gregory Gantner.

▲ *Curl I*, 20" x 24",
©1999, private collection

Photo by Gregory Gantner.

F orget-Me-Not was creat-
ed for The Kiss, an invitational exhibit. After many
transformations, the design
evolved into a valentine in true
Victorian style, with leaves, flowers, and hearts. This piece honors
the work of William Morris, the
artist and idealist whose influence in the nineteenth century
triggered the Arts and Crafts
Movement and promoted a
return to the romance and
chivalry of the Gothic Age.
However, I added thorns to
impose the element
of melancholy (and perhaps a
touch of midlife cynicism).

▲ *Forget-Me-Not*, 18" x 24",
©1998, artist's collection.

*Photo by Gregory Gantner.*

▲*Brocade*, 51" x 50",
©1998, private collection.

*Photo by Gregory Gantner.*

Several years ago, the Art Institute of Chicago held a wonderful exhibit of eighteenth-century French and English silks. I was thrilled by the vibrant, asymmetrical "bizarre silks," as well as the extravagantly delicate pastel patterns. My favorites, however, were the brocade weaves with fanciful patterns based around repeated wavy stripes. Since attending this show, brocade-like patterns keep appearing in my sketchbook. It was inevitable that these ideas would filter into a quilt.

▲ Seeds, 22" x 23",
©1998, artist's collection.

*Photo by Judy Smith-Kressley.*

My *Seeds* quilt is inspired by the mysterious world of seeds themselves: life in a tiny protective armor, carried on socks, sleeves, and fur to unexpected frontiers. It was clear to me when I finished it that this small quilt has an ominous atmosphere. What kind of trouble will these black seeds unleash?

*Glorious Greens* was made for "Women of Taste," an invitational quilt project sponsored by Girls Incorporated of Alameda County, California, which brought together 50 pairs of quilt artists and prominent chefs and culinary entrepreneurs. Each team exchanged ideas and inspirations, with the goal of creating a quilt as the final result. I was paired with Sarah Stegner, the chef for The Ritz-Carlton in Chicago. Sarah treated my husband and me to her talent one night with what seemed like a twenty-course meal in the elegant dining room of the Chicago Ritz-Carlton. Every course was extraordinary. Each dish had sublime harmonies of flavor and texture.

*Glorious Greens* is a celebration of the living gifts of nature. An enlarged collection of lively and radiant growing greens emphasizes the life we are consuming in order to live. This composition gave me the perfect excuse to include some giant cherry tomatoes, one of Mother Nature's food designs that I have always admired.

*Glorious Greens, 58" x 61",*

T hese small quilts are active with life. The tree of life is surrounded by a dense frame of growing pattern. The colors repeat throughout, although each quilt has its own atmosphere and movement. These close-up views of flora created such a beautifully textured surface that I couldn't resist adding some French knots to enhance the tapestry effect.

*Garden Triptych*, 12" x 12" each, ©1999, private collection.

*Photos by Gregory Gantner.*

design
design

## THE GATHERING OF IDEAS AND THE SKETCHBOOK

Today, each quilt begins with an inkling of an idea; a brief glimpse of a composition appears in my head. However, that idea has usually been subconsciously incubating and nursed along for a while on the pages of my sketchbook.

As an artist, it is my job to be inspired all the time, or at least to try to be. Maintaining this level of receptivity and conscious awareness takes constant nurturing. It is not an awful chore—on the contrary, it's a joy! There is inspiration to be found everywhere, and every day, I am on a treasure hunt. I am always looking and exploring for that little something that sparks my imagination or delights my eye.

By recording these fabulous realities in my sketchbook, they become part of my visual encyclopedia, a reference book of ideas that grow in and out of one another, a visual diary of my life.

My sketches are usually simple line drawings of shapes. Shapes have become my symbols and my

language. I am especially attracted to shapes and silhouettes from flowers and plants, and I often draw directly from nature. Even a big city such as Chicago provides endless organic inspiration with its yards, parks, and planter boxes.

Other times I borrow designs from historic decorative objects: carpets, ceramics, textiles, glassware, and fashion. I love a beautifully designed object; whether it's made with precious materials or is a funky folk object, the enjoyment is the same. I get great satisfaction digging through books and visiting museums, making notes on how other artists and cultures have interpreted and stylized forms of nature.

You've probably noticed that certain shapes occur repeatedly in my work: spirals, wiggly lines, spikes, and thorns. Whenever I see a new variation on these motifs, it gets recorded in my sketchbook. I also make notes on color combinations and layout ideas along with words and phrases that spark visual or spiritual images.

Besides a sketchbook, I keep files of clippings from magazines. I am a huge fan of glossy magazines because they bring me new and unexpected images on a monthly basis. They feed my ravenous appetite for new colors, shapes, and ideas. My picture files are organized by category and are treasure-boxes of inspiration.

# MASTER CLASS:
# MOTHER NATURE

Through the ages, artists and designers have been fascinated by the boundless varieties of fauna and flora with which Mother Nature has blessed us. Flowers, especially, have been an integral part of art history. They are earth's ornaments and therefore are symbolic of some of the strongest human emotions. They have been personified in poems and sentimentalized in songs. Flowers participate in the ceremonies and celebrations of almost every culture on earth.

Flowers can be copied directly from nature with photographic precision, or they can be analyzed and enjoyed for their geometrical symmetry and mathematical organization. I am more interested to see how the image is translated through the senses of an artist and into his head, heart, and hands.

Architectural ornament. Louis H. Sullivan.

Throughout my life, I have been drawn to the work of other artists who have the same desire to glorify and reinterpret the ephemeral designs of nature. I find the greatest pleasure in studying decorative design and ornament. The very nature of decorative design requires that the subject (such as a flower or a leaf) be rearranged and manipulated to fit a particular purpose and medium, as with a border on a plate, the pattern of a textile, or the carved cornerstone of a building. The final design must be suitable for its application and therefore must be thoughtfully and skillfully designed.

The design process of simplifying and manipulating is called stylization. The original object is reduced to cartoon-like simplicity to capture its essence and energy. It is both a whittling away and an exaggerating of the characteristics to make an idealized interpretation.

Ornamental door

French Art Nouveau tile

Hand-painted Arts and Crafts vase

## BEGINNING TO "SEE" BY OBSERVING MOTHER NATURE

Before we jump into designing and stylizing, we must first train ourselves to "see." Nothing is better for your powers of observation than the personal study of Mother Nature, herself, especially if you're interested in translating her gifts into your own creations.

I've discovered that the most exceptional decorative artists begin their design process with first-hand observation of fresh flowers and growing plants. Only after a thorough study of the plant

and its outstanding characteristics do they begin to play with and reinterpret these elements. So, let us begin at the source, Mother Nature.

She is designing for a purpose, too. Each living and growing thing has a job to do in the universe, and it's designed to be perfectly suited for the job. Consequently, each creation is designed with a few bold and distinctive characteristics. This consistent uniformity among species enables us to distinguish one from another.

As an artist, it is not necessary to know why a plant or animal exists; it's enough to appreciate the mysterious natural forces that make it look and act as it does. It's often this mystery that we celebrate when making art. We try to re-create the powerful life force and creativity that radiates from every living thing.

Even though we are overwhelmed by the variety of nature's output, we observe that there are visual themes and patterns that occur at every level of life, from the microscopic to the cosmic. These patterns are the designs of life, the shapes of energy and growth. Let's focus our attention on these living patterns so we'll be able to fill our designs with life, too.

# CIRCLES, SPHERES & SPIRALS

Mother Nature is graceful; her universe is made of smooth and gradual curves. The planets, the sun, and the moon are spheres. They revolve around one another in circular orbits. A seedling unfurls itself from the tiny round pod toward the warm sphere of the sun. A pastel bud unwinds itself to reveal its round head of glory. A fern unwraps its spiral of new tightly packed leaves.

# WAVY LINES

Mother Nature is flexible. Her lines undulate with natural momentum. Rivers coil like snakes through rolling hills. Water and sand ripple. The gently bending branches of the willow tree sway in the breeze. The morning glory quietly twines around its arbor. A baby is attached to its mother by a winding cord of life until she is ready to breathe on her own. Gentle slopes and graceful curves are the movement of patient growth.

# RADIATION

Mother Nature is explosive. Her enthusiasm can be ferocious. The sun radiates light and heat. The earth absorbs the heat and bursts into life. Spring erupts, flowers shoot up, their petals thrust unapologetically toward the sky. Spiky seeds spear unsuspecting passersby. The feathers of a peacock fan out into an explosion of emerald.

# VEINS AND BRANCHES

Mother Nature is an engineer. Veins are the highways of life. They carry water and nutrients from roots to trunk to twig. They deliver blood to the tips of your toes. A river is a vein with its tributaries and creeks. The veins of a leaf become a skeleton of structural support.

By looking at plants a layer at a time, it's easier to single out the relationships, patterns, shapes, and textures that occur over and over in living and growing things. Begin by examining the skeleton of a plant and the network of branches that support it. This system of stems has a special pattern of growth. It's a highway branching out at regular intervals. This skeleton creates the form and foundation for the rest of its growth.

The next layer of growth includes leaves, flowers, fruits, and nuts. I find the study of leaves particularly fascinating. The same distinguished kinship between individual parts applies here, too. Each plant is assigned a leaf of a distinctive shape, size, texture, and color. A leaf is like a fingerprint, proclaiming its identity beyond a doubt.

## LEAVES

After a lot of looking, you begin to realize that nature keeps to a limited range of basic shapes and silhouettes, but within that confinement, there is a delightfully endless variety. In this section, we will limit ourselves to the study of leaves because they are obvious examples of this idea. Following are the four basic shapes of leaves. Obviously, there are many variations of each type.

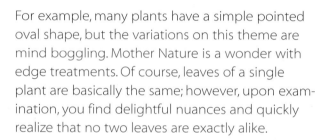

For example, many plants have a simple pointed oval shape, but the variations on this theme are mind boggling. Mother Nature is a wonder with edge treatments. Of course, leaves of a single plant are basically the same; however, upon examination, you find delightful nuances and quickly realize that no two leaves are exactly alike.

The textures of leaves are just as powerfully distinctive as their silhouettes. They can be smooth and shiny, rough and knobby, or sharp and prickly. The color of leaves is also a definite identifier. The range of natural color is outstanding, from black-purples to silvery-whites.

After studying leaves, you may notice that they grow from stems in specific patterns as well. Some grow all on one side of the stem, some sprout alternately on opposite sides of the stem, while others grow directly opposite each other. Some leaves change sizes gradually on a single stem, while some remain the same. Vein patterns of leaves are also quite individual. Some leaves are identifiable solely because of their unique veining pattern.

I am so enamored by the vast variety of leaves, that they have become more and more dominant in my work. I like to keep records of their shapes by placing fresh and pliable leaves directly onto the copy machine for almost-photographic records. I bind them into notebooks for ongoing inspiration.

## Exercise:
# AN EXERCISE IN SEEING

Now that you have accustomed yourself to observing the patterns of nature, it's time to get more specific and involved. We begin to see what we've been looking at with the help of pencil and paper.

First, choose a plant that you love. Think about it. What plant never fails to take your breath away? Prepare to find it—in your garden, a nursery, or the conservatory. It's easier to study a plant when you can handle it or move around it. Your observations are more emotionally charged if you are studying from real life, because you are absorbing other characteristics, like its smell and feel or the environment around it.

What is it about this plant that appeals to you? Why do you feel so strongly about it? This is a simple question, but I'll bet the answer is more complex. You may have emotional as well as visual reasons for liking this plant. Was it in your grandmother's garden or given to you by your first sweetheart? Or, if you're like me, you may choose a plant because it looks like it could star in a horror film.

Really look at the plant. Give yourself the gift of time. Study it from all angles, from above and below. The more you look, the more you will find. Begin to make pencil sketches of all the individual features of the plant, but not necessarily the whole plant. Draw the shape of the leaf, the joints of the stem, count the petals. Draw back views and undersides as well.

Don't panic. These don't need to be elegant drawings, only good observations.

PRACTICE

Don't worry about the quality of your drawings yet. You are just noting the characteristics of your plant and the sketches are a way to help you see them more completely. Sometimes it's helpful to do some simple physical movement, such as stretching or jumping, to loosen up your head and hands. Work big, not tight and small. You will begin to notice the basic shapes, angles, and movement that give the plant its individuality.

If you keep doing this easy observing exercise, over time you will begin to notice the unique details of plants automatically. You will become familiar with nature's principles of growth and eventually be able to apply these principles to your own designs.

You will realize that all forget-me-nots have five petals and that strawberry leaves have wonderfully scalloped edges. By recording these discoveries, they become a valuable reference for later use, especially in the winter months when forget-me-nots and strawberries are not around.

## Exercise:
# PAPER INSTEAD OF PENCIL

Another exercise for sharpening your powers of observation is a simple paper cutting technique. This is especially good for people who find the very thought of drawing inhibiting or for skilled artists who have a difficult time stepping beyond the literal translations of objects. Put away the pencil and get out paper and scissors (or an X-Acto knife) instead.

Study a plant thoroughly and determine its most interesting and unique characteristics. Try to reproduce what you see by cutting directly into the paper with your scissors.

The finer the paper and scissors, the finer amount of detail is possible. Don't be discouraged if your work is somewhat crude. This lack of precision is actually an advantage for continuing on to the next stage of creating your own design.

Cutting paper will help you to see the shapes that make a plant unique. Try cutting out individual leaves, stems, and petals, then go inside these silhouettes to add details such as veins.

The cut paper technique is also helpful for showing the value of the negative spaces of the design. Negative space is the area surrounding the outline of objects and the spaces between them. Negative space can be as important as positive space or the object itself. It also increases one's knowledge of flat pattern and stylized shapes.

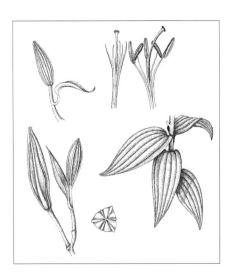

# DESIGN DISCLAIMER

We live in a time when many artists consciously undermine every rule they have learned in order to make a visual statement outrageous enough to force people's attention, perhaps even irreverent enough to introduce a new awareness into a closed mind. Consequently, some very ugly work can be powerful art. The absence of beauty has become a valid form of artistic expression in this age of extremes.

However valid this form of expression may be, I was not born to emphasize the ugly things in our world. I was born with a desire to make beautiful objects that celebrate the wonders of the universe and our place in it. I believe that this desire is a directive from my soul and just as valuable and necessary as exposing the warts of the world. In fact, the more aware I am of the obscene greed and excesses of human beings and the hideous

atrocities that result from them, the more committed I am to add weight to the positive side of the human scale.

I believe that the human spirit can be elevated by beauty. The earth is a heavy planet and holds on tightly to its souls. This is why people need beauty to raise them out of the mud and lift their eyes toward the sun, if only for a moment.

When I talk about good design, please remember that beauty is a very personal concept. Remember, too, that I am celebrating the human spirit and the wonders of the universe. My intention is to make beautiful objects for our own enlightenment. My inspiration comes from Mother Nature and other objects and ornaments inspired by her. Consequently, the ideas found in this book are based on traditional concepts of nature-oriented design and decoration because these are the foundation of my work. It's not my intention to dictate rules, but to share guidelines that have directed me on my path.

# WHAT IS GOOD DESIGN?

Design by definition is a conscious arrangement of form, line, and color. Conscious arrangement means the design has been thoughtfully prepared and the elements arranged in some orderly or unified fashion. A successful design doesn't happen by chance; it takes some thought and time to prepare.

A good design expresses life, invention, and individuality. It shows the unique skills and preferences of its maker.

A good design should be simplified enough that its meaning is easily grasped. Simplifying your design refers to the process of filtering out visual elements that detract from your overall idea or are unsuitable for your medium. It does not pertain to the emotional content of your work. By sifting out unnecessary elements, the emotion you convey can actually become more concentrated and powerful.

The phrase "easily grasped" doesn't mean that a successful design must be mundane or shallow. It means that the basic idea must be readily available for the viewer to discover, not buried in confusion and overburdened by technique.

As designers begin working out ideas on paper, they must be mindful of the ultimate medium they are designing for. Every medium has its own particular beauty as well as its limitations, whether it is wood, metal, glass, or fiber. Designers should have respect for the materials and the craftsmanship it requires. They should take advantage of the medium's unique characteristics and illuminate them.

Designers should translate the inherent beauty of the original idea into a design that can be realized with ease in whatever medium they are using. They should not expect the materials or the craftsman to do what is unreasonably difficult or impossible.

As quilt artists, we have the advantage of being both the designer and the craftsman for our creations. We already have respect for our materials and probably some working knowledge of the physical characteristics of fabric and thread. However, there is a wide variety of experience in the field of art quilting. Some of us began as artists and discovered quilting along the way. Others began as seamstresses and became attracted to the opportunities for self-expression in quilting. There is no doubt that there is something for all of us to learn.

Anyone who wants to translate their ideas into fabric needs to practice. It takes thought, skill, and patience to take full advantage of the medium of fabric and thread.

## DESIGNING BEGINS

Designing begins with your first drawing and ends with your last stitch. You must think creatively throughout the work, for there is much to consider along the way. The constant selecting, altering, and editing that goes on throughout the work is an essential part of designing. Be flexible, allow yourself to deviate from the original plan, and don't continue until you've reached a satisfactory solution. In other words, don't be easily satisfied.

Allow yourself the time to do a thorough job as you are designing and constructing. It's better to do one great job than three half-hearted ones. The weak projects will scowl at you whenever you see them, but the energy generated by a good design will reflect back on you and be worth the effort.

## Exercise: SIMPLIFYING WHAT YOU SEE

At this point you've studied a plant in minute detail and from all angles. Don't forget to identify why you are attracted to it. You've made sketches or cut paper studies of the most interesting aspects of your plant. Now comes the fun part—designing. This is when you start trading places with Mother Nature. She has inspired you, and now it is your turn to transform that energy into your own creation.

In order to translate your collection of plant studies into a well-planned design and eventually into fabric and thread, the forms must be simplified. The plant studies are a point of departure from which we can exaggerate the decorative details, such as leaf edges and petal folds.

It takes practice to cultivate an ability to design comfortably and consciously. One easy way to begin manipulating your natural forms is by selecting the most interesting features of your plant and reducing them to basic geometric shapes.

Look at your plant. What shapes do you see? Circles? Squares? Triangles? Now draw it using only those shapes, without detail. This drawing may seem ridiculously simple, but this exercise will help you define the individual units for the eventual translation of your design into fabric.

These basic shapes can be transformed further by enlarging, reducing, and repositioning in order to change the emphasis of the composition. In other words, exaggerate the individual shapes. Keep in mind that you're not making a photographic copy, so you don't need permission to make these changes.

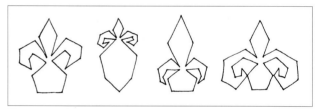

The same shapes are used in each drawing, but each has a different area exaggerated.

Simplified drawings of an iris using basic geometric shapes

## Exercise: CONSCIOUS ARRANGEMENT

You have identified the shapes that make up your natural forms and started to exaggerate them. The following exercise allows you to experiment and expand on what you've done.

Draw several circles, squares, and triangles at least 6" in diameter. Now try to arrange your plant to fit inside these shapes. This artificial frame will force you to single out or select one or two of the most decorative elements to concentrate on, such as a leaf, a bud, or a blossom.

You need to emphasize and exaggerate those elements of the plant in order to fit it into the assigned area. Don't worry about detail. Just use simple lines and shapes for these drawings. Once you get started, you'll find endless arrangement options. Keep working until you have exhausted every possibility.

Forcing your plant to fit into a prescribed area also forces you to think differently. So now you have selected, emphasized, and exaggerated your natural forms and you have started to consciously arrange them. Some of your ideas may even begin to look like quilts. You are designing!

### Getting Down to Details

Now, it's time to get down to details. Create designs as energetic and unique as the plant form that originally inspired you by stylizing the shapes and making them your own. Because each shape will eventually become an independent and movable element in your composition, it is important that each element is carefully formed. Each element is a design in itself, and it's unlikely that a good design can be made with ill-formed pieces.

Draw a plant to fit into a square, triangle, and circle

Japanese family crests with peonies show many ways to fill a circle using different views and arrangements of the same plant.

## Exercise:
# STYLIZING

The process of departure and simplification from the real plant is called stylization or conventionalization. The degree and look of stylization will vary depending on the artist's mood and preferences. Simplification, distortion, and exaggeration are the keys to stylizing a form. There are endless graphic possibilities within a single shape.

Shown is a dandelion leaf stylized in several different ways. Each one has its own character, style, and mood. The leaf on the left is the most realistic portrayal; the leaves get more cartoon-like with every translation. Each leaf becomes a decorative object and a possible puzzle piece to fit into your final composition.

## Exercise:
# ADDING DEPTH AND INTEREST

Choose a leaf or blossom from your original plant and stylize it in as many ways as possible. The idea is to translate the plant form through your own head, heart, and hands. Distort and exaggerate whatever decorative characteristics your subject has. Intensify the shapes, edges, lines, folds, and veins. Use all of your senses to add layers of depth and interest to your designs. You are making an extreme interpretation and need not be confined to botanical reality. It's more important that your design has the interest, ease, and confidence to stand on its own.

Stylized dandelion
leaf sketches

Shown at right are examples of how other artists have stylized plants. Each artist has taken a single plant and interpreted it several different ways. As you look at these examples, you will begin to see how the decorative arts have influenced my work. There are many classical decorative devices that I have applied to my designs, both consciously and unconsciously. The most notable similarity between these samples and my work is the use of bold graphics, strong contrasts, and sharp lines. Studying these examples will give you new ideas for stylizing your original floral inspiration.

From *Or et Couleurs* by G. Darcy, A. Calavas, Paris, 1920

From *Or et Couleurs* by G. Darcy, A. Calavas, Paris, 1920

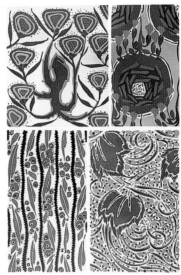

From *Suggestions, 60 Motifs en Couleurs* by E. A. Seguy, Ch. Massin, Paris, 1926

If you wish to study the historic decorative arts, there are many resources available. Several publishers have reproduced some classic encyclopedias of ornament originally printed in the nineteenth and early-twentieth centuries. There are also several new volumes that catalog European and ethnic textile designs. Auction house publications are another great source that lets you see an overview of design history and discover the styles that are personally appealing. There are also a wealth of magazines covering the contemporary and historic decorative arts. Several of these resources are listed on pages 126-127.

Realistic thistle drawing from *A Book of Studies in Plant Form with Some Suggestions for their Application to Design* by A. E. V. Lilley and W. Midgley, 1907

Stylized thistle drawings from *A Book of Studies in Plant Form with Some Suggestions for their Application to Design* by A. E. V. Lilley and W. Midgley, 1907

I find this part of the design stage one of the most exciting in the entire quiltmaking process. By this point, I am really beginning to feel the potential of the idea and its shapes. The inkling becomes a bubbling of anticipation, and I am ready to graduate to a larger format.

This is when I cover my work walls with poster paper and start drawing giant shapes—shapes that were hinted at in those first crude sketches. I use soft, dark pencils or black markers to make the outlines of leaves, blossoms, and spirals. The shapes are perfected with layers of lines until their silhouettes are smooth and the curves gracefully sculpted.

Once the shapes are perfect, I work inside and around them adding details, often using layers of tracing paper so I can try as many variations as possible. It's important to allow your imagination to fly through every spark of possibility and to catch it on paper. Try every variation, cut up your drawings, and combine ideas.

Take advantage of the flexibility of this process while your ideas are still on paper. Nothing is permanent; however, once your ideas have been turned into fabric, it's difficult to rework the shapes. It's best to spend time now to create a wonderful shape on paper. Begin small for your first projects, so you are not overwhelmed.

After a lot of experimenting with details, an attitude takes over and each element absorbs a continuity of style. Continuity of the look or treatment of the elements is important, since they are to be used together in the same composition. They should look as if they have the same origin.

In the following chapters, you will learn that almost any shape can be made into individual fabric units and eventually become part of a quilt.

## MATERIALS

I came to quilting as an artist. When I first discovered quilts, it was their strong graphic designs and bold colors that attracted me. Quilts were large designs in fabric, and I had to figure out how to make them one way or another! The drive to make quilts was so strong that I learned mostly the hard way, by making mistakes.

It was natural to use materials and supplies from my life in art departments rather than my limited time spent in high school home economics class. If I needed to hold something together, glue and tape automatically came to mind. Consequently, many of the techniques presented here have evolved because of my background in the graphic arts.

My techniques have changed over time and within the confines of a limited budget and a constricted space. As a result, I am a very frugal quilter. The materials I use are basic, easy to find, and affordable. It's up to me to use these common materials in a magical way.

I would like to encourage all quilters to get the most use from the materials at hand. There have been so many innovations in quilting supplies that there are many alternative products to try. Experiment with your supplies and try substituting others for the ones I've listed. These are not necessarily the most effective or accessible materials for everyone; they are simply supplies that have worked wonderfully for me for many years.

**Iron-on interfacing:** I prefer Shirtailor® by Pellon®, but you can use another non-woven, medium-weight fusible interfacing.

**Fusible web** (iron-on adhesive): Wonder Under® by Pellon or Aleene's Fusible Web™. Just make sure the fusible web is light- or medium-weight or your quilt will be stiff.

**Glue stick:** Uhu®, small size

**X-Acto knife with a #11 blade**

**Pigma™ Micron pen**

## USING YOUR NATURAL COMPASS

I make natural curves; they are not made with a draftsman's compass or French curve. I use my body as my compass. A compass is a device that holds a center point as a line is drawn equidistant (in a circle) around that fixed center. The center points around which my compass rotates are my joints: the wrist, the elbow, and the shoulder. By moving my hand or arm in its natural arch, I am able to make smooth graceful curves and faultless spirals.

Begin by drawing a free-hand spiral, almost perfect but not quite. Now, use your natural compass to sculpt it into perfection by sweeping over it again and again, not all at once, but sections at a time. Eventually, the layers of lines become one satisfying smooth line.

The size of the circle determines which body parts are used: small curves, the wrist; medium curves, the elbow; large curves, the shoulder. Stretch to limber up before you begin. It just takes practice.

## TWO STYLES OF WORKING

My quilt designs tend toward two different styles. The first consists of designs composed of pre-made shapes, which are arranged instinctually or collaged. The other style consists of formal compositions with very specific relationships between the elements, such as close-up views of a stylized plant with the design features radiating from the center. I'll show you both processes. They are both done in appliqué, but the technique changes according to the composition.

The discovery of appliqué and the ability to make independent, organic shapes has transformed my work. The final composition isn't predetermined; it changes and grows as the fabric shapes are auditioned for their proper arrangement. This collage technique of quiltmaking is satisfying because the autonomous pieces allow for playfulness and unexpected design discoveries.

Each quilt begins with the inkling of an idea. I collect shapes and silhouettes directly from nature and appealing motifs from historical decorative objects. These inspirations are recorded into my sketchbook and begin to brew in my brain. After a while, several shapes will begin to dominate my thoughts. These forms become the inspiration and the subjects for my next quilt. I don't plan a composition in advance; I wait for the shapes to tell me what to do.

Sometimes this period of incubation, of waiting for the shapes to rise to the forefront, can be pure hell. Ironically, this creative limbo between quilts causes more anguish now, after twenty years of quiltmaking, than it used to. Perhaps it's a problem of competing with myself.

On one such frustrating afternoon, I decided to take a short walk to use up some of that undirected, antsy energy. As I walked through my neighborhood, I noticed wonderfully ambitious dandelions everywhere. I have always liked their shape and they appeared to be as restless as I was. These persistent weeds flaunt their divine right to flourish. In their shameless pride, I'm sure they are unaware of their sinister reputation. Their tenacious energy, determination, and powerful life force was certainly worth celebrating. The creative drought was over. I started *Weeds* as soon as I got home.

▲ *Weeds*, 43" x 43", 1998,
private collection.

*Photo by Gregory Gantner.*

# COLLAGE QUILTS: GENERAL CONSTRUCTION TECHNIQUES

1 *Select the subject of your quilt.*

2 *Determine the scale—do you want large or small shapes?*

3 *Determine what the shapes will be.*

4 *Design the shapes and cut patterns from light cardboard.*

5 *Choose your color palette and select fabrics.*

6 *Prepare your shapes using either the raw-edge or turned-edge appliqué method (see page 96).*

7 *Place shapes on a flat surface (design wall, table, or floor) and arrange until you are satisfied with your composition.*

8 *Embroider the independent shapes, stitching through any fusible web. Mark locations of pieces before removing them from your composition so they can be returned to their proper place.*

9 *Attach all the elements. Be systematic, starting with the bottom-most layer and working upward.*

- *Pieces that are backed with fusible web can be ironed on (follow manufacturer's instructions).*

- *Raw edge pieces should be tacked to the background with a small amount of glue stick.*

- *Turned-edge pieces should be pinned in place and then taped into place immediately before sewing them. Don't leave tape on your quilt top overnight.*

10 *Sew the shapes to the background.*

- *For glued pieces, if the glue does not keep its hold, stitch around the edges with a straight stitch, otherwise this step can be skipped. Finish the raw edges with machine embroidery (such as satin stitch).*

- *For turned-edge shapes. Top stitch the pieces in place, removing the tape one piece at a time as the needle approaches. Do not sew through the tape.*

11 *After the thread ends are tied and clipped, cut away the fabric behind the pieces.*

As you read on, you will be able to follow my design and construction process for the *Weeds* quilt. My directions are general, in that I don't give specific yardages or patterns. My intent is to encourage you to practice your own design skills and develop your own set of unique shapes and symbols for your art quilts; to rely on your own creative resources instead of repeating an existing design. By following the sequence of steps, you can apply this process of design and construction to your individual appliquéd quilt ideas.

Begin sewing only after the elements are in their right places and you are happy with the composition. Each quilt will go together differently depending on the particular design, but the basic construction techniques are the same.

# COLLAGE *WEEDS* QUILT: BEGINNING

## Determine the Scale
The first step toward making a collage quilt such as *Weeds* is determining its scale. Should there be a lot of fussy little leaves or large dramatic shapes? Will the leaves be 6" or 24"? For me, only a large scale could capture the uninhibited creativity of this triumphant plant.

## Determine the Shapes
What other shape could be combined with the dandelion leaf? Since the dandelion leaf is sharp and spiky, it would be nice to include an opposing shape, something smooth and round. A spiral is a perfect contrast and will also add to the feeling of energy and growth that I want to create. Two to four shapes are plenty for me to work with in one composition. Any more make the design too cluttered and confusing.

Real dandelion leaves and fabric leaves

## Design Shapes & Cut Patterns

To accentuate the feeling of energetic growth, I made each leaf from two gracefully curving halves. The negative space between the halves becomes a vein, which helps break up the large mass of the leaves and adds direction and movement to the quilt. The size and angle of curve varies within each leaf set. The spirals are irregular, which gives them an active exuberance. It's important that each element is well designed, for they all must contribute their full strength to the overall design. After I've designed my shapes, I cut light cardboard patterns.

## Choose a Palette

Next, I choose a color palette. Since green is the color of growth, I chose fabrics from light acid green to deep forest green, plus two tobacco colors for interest.

Color palette for *Weeds*

## Raw-Edge or Turned-Edge Appliqué?

To transform the shapes into fabric, I first determine which appliqué technique will work best for each shape. I use two different appliqué styles, depending on the element's shape and size. One involves a turned-edge finish that is eventually top-stitched into place. The other technique is a raw-edged method that is later finished with embroidery. Both methods use a medium-weight iron-on interfacing (originally intended for shirt tailoring) as a backing.

I usually reserve raw-edge appliqué for shapes that can be easily maneuvered through the sewing machine: pieces with simple curves and straight lines or shapes with a lot of points. I use the turned-edge technique for large shapes that have very smooth, voluptuous curves.

I made the dandelion leaves with raw edges. I can make wonderfully sharp points with raw edge appliqué if I finish the edges with a satin stitch. On the other hand, I made the spirals using turned-edge appliqué, since this technique creates very smooth curves. It's much easier to attach a spiral with a straight stitch than it is to control a satin stitch while the spiral is maneuvered through the sewing machine.

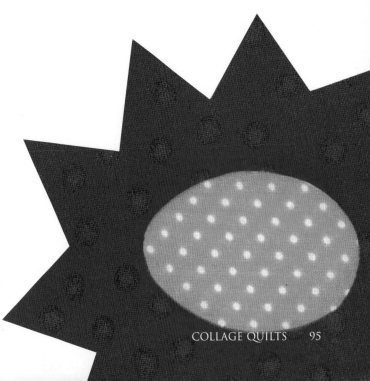

## BASIC APPLIQUÉ TECHNIQUES

### Raw-Edge Appliqué

1 *Trace the pattern onto the non-adhesive side of the iron-on interfacing (remember that images need to be reversed).*

2 *Using a sharp X-Acto blade, cut the interfacing just outside of the drawn line.*

3 *Adhere the cut shapes to the back of your fabric following the directions for your type of interfacing.*

4 *Using a sharp X-Acto blade, cut the fused fabric and interfacing on the line.*

5 *Arrange on a fabric background.*

### Turned-Edge Appliqué

1 *Trace the pattern onto the non-adhesive side of the iron-on interfacing (remember that images need to be reversed).*

2 *Using a sharp X-Acto blade, cut the interfacing exactly on the drawn line.*

3 *Adhere the cut shapes to the back of your fabric following the directions for your type of interfacing.*

4 *Cut the fabric ¼" outside the interfacing shape.*

5 *Clip at least every ¼", cutting almost to the interfacing. Clip closer together for tighter curves.*

6 *Finger-press the fabric over the edge of the interfacing, then press with an iron.*

7 *Lift away the fabric from the interfacing. Apply washable glue stick sparingly to interfacing under the fabric and press down into place.*

8 *Arrange on a fabric background.*

## RAW-EDGE APPLIQUÉ

### Trace the Shapes

Using a very fine permanent fabric marker, I trace sharp-edged shapes onto the non-adhesive side of a medium-weight iron-on interfacing. I trace the leaf patterns twice, once top side up, and also reversed, so there are several sets of leaves to work with. Then, I cut the interfacing leaves just outside the drawn line. Next, I adhere the interfacing shapes to the back of the appropriate fabric using an iron with steam. Lastly, using a sharp, new X-Acto blade, I cut the fused fabric and interfacing, on the line, to the finished leaf size.

Cut leaf shapes with an X-Acto knife

Iron-on interfacing adds strength and body to the fabric shape. The interfacing also allows me to cut away the extra unseen layers of fabric behind the large appliquéd units. Cutting away the extra fabric layers leaves the final quilt pliable and, for the most part, a single layer of fabric plus interfacing. I reserve using fusible web for very small raw-edged shapes. After the leaves have been traced and cut, I move on to make the spirals.

# TURNED-EDGE APPLIQUÉ

I made the spirals using the turned-edge appliqué technique. A characteristic of turned-edge appliqué is that it actually raises above the background, adding a feeling of dimension and depth to the layers. This relief-quality can be used to your advantage within your design. I use a system for turned-edge appliqué similar to the traditional freezer-paper method, but instead of removable freezer-paper templates, I use iron-on interfacing templates, which remain inside the quilt. This extra interfacing adds a welcome strength and body in quilts that are meant to hang crisply on a wall instead of drape over a bed or a person. Iron-on interfacing can be cut with precision and creates an edge that is strong enough to fold fabric over.

## Trace the Patterns

I trace around the cardboard patterns directly onto the non-adhesive side of the interfacing using a fine permanent fabric marker or, if backing light-colored fabrics, a pencil. I always trace more shapes than I will probably need, especially for favorite shapes that I will surely use in the future.

## Cut Out the Pieces

Using an X-Acto knife, I cut out the interfacing shapes exactly on the tracing line. These pieces need to be cut precisely, because any lumps and bumps around the edge will show in the final product. An X-Acto knife works well for cutting interfacing, giving clean, smooth lines. I then iron the interfacing shapes to the back of the proper fabric using a steam setting. Always check to see that all interfacing edges are tightly adhered.

Finished spirals

## Clip Around Shape

I cut the fabric ¼" outside the interfacing shape. This ¼" of extra fabric eventually gets folded to the back to create the finished piece. However, before the edge can be turned, it must be clipped. With scissors at a right angle to the edge, I clip every ¼" around the entire shape. I cut almost to the interfacing, but not quite. As in traditional appliqué, you need to clip closer together for tight curves and looser for soft curves. Progress is slow at first, but eventually a rhythm develops. Small, well-sharpened scissors make this job much easier. After the entire shape is clipped, I gently fold the fabric to the back with my fingers, using the interfacing as a guide. The resulting fringe gives the iron something to catch hold of. Next, I carefully iron the fringe over the interfacing. Ideally, the fringe should fold like a deck of cards. I work in sections, so I'm not working against myself.

## Press the Pieces

Now, I lightly press the fabric tabs to the back. Gently, I run my finger under the fringe to lift it away from the interfacing. I apply washable glue stick sparingly to the interfacing, under the fringe. I use an all-purpose paper glue stick that you can get at any office supply store. Glue sticks from fabric stores tend to be too soft and messy. I then finger-press the fringe back into place and reposition any tab that is out of place. Once the entire edge is neatly attached, I iron it, this time on the top side. This way I can check for imperfections and keep my iron glue-free. At this point, I reposition tabs that are out of alignment. Covering the ironing board helps avoid getting excess glue on it. When the spiral is finished, it is ready to use. Turned-edge appliqué is quite sturdy and also very portable.

Turned-edge spirals in progress

## NEGATIVE SHAPES

One of the most entertaining features of working with appliqué is the bonus shapes that are created in the process. These are the negative shapes, or the surrounding shapes, which have been cut away. These cut-away shapes are often as good, if not better, than the original shape.

A leaf and a spiral with their negative shapes

You can end up with bonus shapes with both appliqué techniques. After you cut a spiral, you also have a spiral left over. When you cut away a leaf's vein, the vein becomes an object in itself and can be used in a design. Becoming aware of negative shapes can add wonderful and unexpected elements to your design vocabulary.

## BACKGROUND

Now I have a pile of leaves and a stack of spirals, but I need a background to arrange them on. I usually begin with a solid color or a very simple, unobtrusive print for background fabric. White, gray, or black provide the high contrast that I prefer between elements. For *Weeds*, I decided that black fabric would look best, perhaps suggesting black Midwestern soil. The dark background also makes the colored leaves and spirals more vibrant and lively. I also prefer to use a heavyweight cotton background fabric, such as cotton duck or sheeting. These fabrics are tough and can withstand a lot of machine embroidery and quilting without buckling or shrinking.

## PLAYTIME

Instead of designing my quilt on a wall, I know from experience that it's wiser to work on a table when making smaller quilts. The long, large dandelion leaves and curly spirals would be difficult to manipulate on a wall, and a lot of pins are needed to hold each shape in place. Often good ideas evaporate in the time it takes to pin and unpin pieces. Working on a table allows for a faster and more spontaneous arranging of elements because you have gravity to assist in holding the awkward pieces in place. Spontaneity is important during first encounters between new elements because it's essential to experiment with as many relationships and compositions as possible.

Arranging leaves and spirals

## BONUS SHAPES SAVE THE DAY

Sometimes shapes get rejected from a project altogether. Even though this can be discouraging, it's not a disaster. I simply save these shapes for the future. There is no doubt that they'll be perfect in some other quilt. Occasionally, I even make fabric shapes just for fun, with no specific purpose in mind. These free agents are available for any future ideas. The blue flowers in the *Weeds* quilt are just such shapes. After arranging the leaves and spirals, I could tell some other element was needed.

Blue flowers added to leaves and spirals

There is always a point when working on a collage quilt when I bring out the orphaned shapes to see if they can find a home in a new composition. While sifting through my collection of shapes, I came across a bag of stylized flowers. I auditioned several styles and colors, but it wasn't until the blue flowers had their turn that the quilt began to sing. The perfect addition! The flowers are raw edged and already backed with fusible web, not interfacing. This works because they are relatively small units. Chance and accident are main players when working spontaneously. Sometimes I make a quilt composed of nothing but leftovers and orphans with quite delightful and surprising results.

## NATURAL RELATIONSHIPS

Arranging the collage pieces is the most exciting part of the quiltmaking process. All efforts thus far have been directed toward this point. We design exciting elements so they will be even more exciting when put together. Because the combination of new elements creates a power that you only imagined up until now, it is extremely important to give this process your full attention.

It is also the most spontaneous part of the process, but keep in mind that the perfect arrangement never happens on the first try. Finding the perfect composition is rarely automatic. In fact, finding the proper composition is guaranteed to take me several days for a small quilt and weeks for a large piece. Fine tuning a design can be stressful because I want to test all the design options. This is also why nothing gets attached, fused, or sewn until all possibilities are tested. There is nothing worse than stopping short of the ideal arrangement and then discovering the answer when it's too late to apply it. Again, give this process all the time it takes to solve the problem.

You must become extremely sensitive to the natural relationships between shapes. Learn to feel the movement and flow that develops as shapes interact. Shift and shuffle shapes until the most powerful graphic statement evolves. Since it's my goal to celebrate the creativity of Mother Nature and the power of the life force, I am constantly looking for interactions that create movement and energy.

Over time, recognizing natural relationships becomes easier, especially if you let Mother Nature be your guide. Every natural object, whether it be a rock or a tree, was made for a purpose. Consequently, each object is made to a specific set of rules. This is why rose quartz always looks like rose quartz and a red oak is unmistakable for any other tree. Rules give continuity to all natural objects and pattern to our world.

Artists must also assign a set of "rules to grow by" to give their composition organization. Without rules, a collage will be chaotic and senseless. Nature repeats the same rules of organization throughout the natural world; basic shapes and patterns are repeated continually in different forms.

**Repeating Shapes.** Groupings of similar shapes give pattern to the natural world.

**Parallelism.** Lines and shapes often repeat themselves at regular intervals creating natural harmony.

**Radiation.** Radiation is one of Mother Nature's favorite organizing devices, especially in the plant world. Lines, shapes, and color grow from a central source.

**Regularly Diminishing.** This device of natural organization is seen everywhere. For example, as things grow, they are larger at the base and gradually get smaller the further away they are from its source.

**Balance and Symmetry.** An even distribution of weight is another principle that adds order to the world.

**Regularly Changing.** Like regularly diminishing, Mother Nature makes small but regular changes to create a smooth transition between the lines and shapes or colors of an object. Leaves on a branch often change color gradually with the freshest and brightest colors seen on the newest growth.

These organizing principles may seem obvious. It's easy to see these organizing principles in the natural world, but these simple relationships must be consciously internalized by designers to make their designs look as effortless as Mother Nature's.

Assorted bonus and leftover shapes

For *Weeds*, I applied all of nature's organizing principles, although subconsciously. Plus, I assigned some of my own rules, since this is an imaginary garden. The dandelion leaves radiate toward the center instead of away from it. The spirals form the base from which each long leaf sprouts. They also support a series of smaller leaves and create a frame around the composition. These are my self-imposed "rules to grow by" that give this quilt some continuity and logic. Organizing so many elements becomes much easier when you have a constant formula to follow. I encourage you to create some of your own "rules to grow by" for your designs.

# CONSTRUCTION OF *WEEDS*

After getting all the elements arranged exactly as I want them, I begin to sew.

Before I start attaching shapes to the background, I complete as much embroidery on the small independent sections as possible. It's much easier to manipulate a small unit in the sewing machine than a large quilt top.

## Embroider Independent Shapes

The only independent shapes that require embroidery, other than what is used to attach the shapes to the background, are the centers of the blue flowers. Small circular shapes like these are especially nice to embroider ahead of time. I keep the paper backing on the flowers (and any other shapes backed with fusible web) until I'm ready to fuse them in place. This makes the pieces sturdier and more manageable. It also means that embroidery is stitched right through the paper lining. The sewing lines simply perforate the paper and make it easier to peel away later.

Working with one flower at a time, I make small dots on the background fabric with a white pencil so the flower can be replaced exactly. After each flower is embroidered with a zigzag stitch, I peel away the paper backing and place the flowers back into their proper positions.

## Attach the Elements

The next step is to attach all the elements to the background without disturbing the composition. These pieces cannot be sewn into place until their edges are tacked in place. I approach this process starting with the bottom-most layer of appliqué and work upward.

Top with leaves glued on

### (1) The Flowers

I begin with the blue flowers. They are one of the bottom layers of appliqué because they sit directly on the background fabric and they don't overlap any other units. The flowers are backed with fusible web, so they can simply be fused into place with an iron. Embroidery can wait until the leaves are also attached.

### (2) The Leaves

Next, I fix the dandelion leaves into position. The background is subtly marked before each leaf is removed so I can reposition them exactly. Since they are not backed with adhesive, they have to be tacked to the background with a small amount of glue stick. Attaching one leaf section at a time, I make sure that the edges are well adhered.

Once all leaves are glued into place, I temporarily attach the spirals and simple leaves with straight pins. Temporarily tacking down the spirals allows the dandelion leaves to be stitched into place, their edges finished with embroidery, and the underlying background fabric trimmed away before the spirals are permanently top stitched. It also enables me to stitch the embroidery onto the edges of the leaves continuously, without stopping and starting when a spiral overlaps, which would otherwise interrupt its path. I remove the pins as I work.

I stitch each leaf to the background with a matching straight stitch, working very close to the leaf's edge. I then finish the leaves with embroidery: in this case, a simple but effective satin stitch. I choose darker colors of thread for the inner lines of the leaf and lighter threads on all their edges. Using contrasting colors of thread adds depth to the center vein and makes the edges glow. I pull the thread ends to the back, knot them, and clip them. Now is the time to also finish the edges of the blue flowers.

Working from the backside of the quilt top, I cut away the black fabric behind the leaves. This makes the quilt easier to handle and allows the colors to be their brightest. I neatly trim the black fabric as close to the line of stitching as possible.

### (3) The Spirals

Now, I attach the spirals. Working with one spiral at a time, I remove the pins of the first spiral and position the spiral perfectly into place, making sure it is flat and smooth. The spiral is tacked into place using small pieces of masking tape.

The spiral is top stitched into place, removing the tape a piece at a time as the needle approaches. After the ends are tied, I cut away the fabric behind the spirals, including the leaf sections that overlapped. The small leaves are aligned with their spirals and fused into place. I finish the leaves with embroidery. The top is complete.

Top with spiral taped on

## THE COLLAGE PROCESS IN SUMMARY

Using the collage technique is a very satisfying way to work. When you begin to work, there is no obvious outcome, and the elements often proceed to take you on a sensual adventure. This journey always has its highlights and discoveries, as well as discouragement and despair. To do your best work, you must be willing to ride each phase to a satisfying solution.

Cultivate a feeling for the natural relationships between shapes and colors and learn to react quickly and spontaneously as the relationships happen. Be willing to try unexpected combinations and give up "easy answers" to reach the next level of visual excitement. An artist is an explorer of the senses; the collage technique allows for an interesting expedition every time.

*Iris*, 30" x 32½", 1999.

# formal quilts

The formal style of working can be just as adventurous as the collage technique. A formal quilt begins with a definite drawing from which patterns are made. However, as the design evolves, changing your preconceived idea is natural and acceptable.

My formal quilts are usually interpretations of definite flowers, so the individual petals are specifically designed and constructed to radiate from a center. Aside from this structure, the design discipline stops here. I make the flower units as separate appliqué pieces so they can be rearranged and repositioned spontaneously. Examples of my formal quilts are *Lily*, *Wild Flower*, and *Gloriosa* (all shown on page 60).

Materials used for the formal style of appliqué are identical to the materials for collage quilts, but having a formal starting point and a definite relationship between shapes causes the sequence of decisions to be slightly different.

## FORMAL *IRIS* QUILT: BEGINNING

It must be obvious that I am quite impressed by irises. Their shape is wonderfully complicated, a perfect plant to study for details. Their leaves grow in a flat sheet of alternating spears. Their stems zig and zag at each point of new growth. Their proud heads are held high and noble, with a curly mane. They have extraordinary engineering. As fingers clasp together, they have three petals reaching up and three reaching down. Their colors can be sublime, from black and periwinkle to yellow, brown, and pure white. Their beauty is illusive; the delicate papery blossom lasts but a few days and wilts quickly if picked. Of course, something must be done to honor this wavy wonder. Designing must begin!

# FORMAL QUILTS: GENERAL CONSTRUCTION TECHNIQUES

**1** Select the subject of your quilt.

**2** Make a very clean outline drawing of your composition. This is your master drawing for patterns.

**3** Determine the individual units for construction.

**4** Create a tracing for each unit so you can map out each one individually.

**5** Determine the pattern pieces within each unit.

**6** Use your pattern to cut plastic templates. Mark the front side.

**7** Choose your color palette and select fabrics.

**8** Prepare your shapes using the raw-edge or turned-edge appliqué technique (see page 96). If your design is symmetrical, each pattern is traced twice, once face up and once face down.

**9** Place shapes on a flat surface (design wall, table, or floor).

**10** Assemble each unit one layer at a time using your tracings as the placement guide. Stitch units together.

**11** Place completed units on a flat surface and arrange them. Try variations until you are satisfied with the final composition.

**12** If you have not yet selected background fabric, do so now.

**13** Create tracings for the background shapes by outlining the empty spaces, allowing an extra ½" to 1" on all sides.

**14** Draw a master tracing of the final composition.

**15** Cut and prepare the background pieces. Tuck them underneath your shapes.

**16** Embroider small independent pieces.

**17** Attach all the elements. Be systematic, starting with the bottom-most layer and working upward.

- Pieces that are backed with fusible web can be ironed on (follow manufacturer's instructions).

- Raw-edge pieces should be tacked to the background with a small amount of glue stick.

- Turned-edge pieces should be pinned in place and then taped into place immediately before sewing them. Don't leave tape on your quilt top overnight.

**18** Sew the shapes to the background.

- For glued pieces, if the glue does not keep its hold, stitch around the edges with a straight stitch, otherwise this step can be skipped. Finish the raw edges with machine embroidery (such as satin stitch).

- For turned-edge shapes. Topstitch the pieces in place, removing the tape one piece at a time as the needle approaches. Do not sew through the tape.

**19** After the thread ends are tied and clipped, cut away the fabric behind the pieces.

After making many sketches, the iris evolved into a formal design, a symmetrical close-up view of the flower, emphasizing the central fuzzy beard and the curly petals. The drawing reads as an iris, but it is stylized and reduced into the bare essence of the flower.

Beginning the iris drawing

Iris drawing in progress

Final iris drawing

## Create a Pattern Guide

The first step in transforming an idea into fabric is to make a very clean outline drawing of the composition. This master drawing serves as the guide for planning the patterns and determining the layers of construction.

## Determine the Units

Next, I determine the individual units for construction. Even though I am working from a definite design, I still want to leave every chance to explore new design options through the entire process. For example, making each petal of the flower as an independent unit allows me the freedom to play with their positions in the final composition.

## Trace the Units

I then create a tracing for each unit. Since I want the petals to radiate from behind the center of the flower, I extend the lines of each petal so it can eventually be tucked underneath the center. I also lengthen the lines of the bottom petal beyond the edges of the drawing, again to allow for possible variations in the final composition.

Trace separate petal units

Bottom petal

## Determine the Pattern Pieces

Now that each unit has been identified and drawn separately, it's time to determine the pattern pieces within each petal. When working in this type of formal composition, I construct my quilts in overlapping layers instead of using traditional seamed techniques. These layers are held together with various kinds of satin stitches or other embroidery, so I must determine which areas are overlapping and which ones are tucked underneath their neighbors. These iris petals are a series of shapes that echo one another, so it's not difficult to determine the layering sequence. Notice where the template pieces overlap.

Top petal

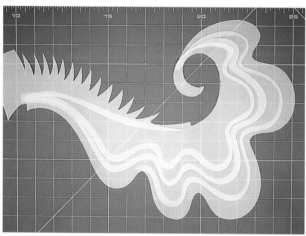

Plastic template pieces showing ¼" overlap of the middle petal

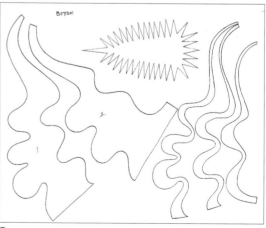

Middle petal

I draw dotted lines on the individual petal tracings to indicate where each piece will tuck under its neighbor. Each section is traced separately, including the extra overlapping area. Since the design is symmetrical and both halves are identical, only one side of the design needs to be traced.

Bottom pieces

## Create Reusable Templates

I make reusable templates from these patterns by placing a sheet of template plastic over the pattern and cutting it out with an X-Acto knife. I mark the surface of each to indicate the front side of the template.

## Choose the Palette

After many years of collecting, I now have shelves of fabric to choose from when making a quilt. For the *Iris* quilt, I decide to work with a palette of purples, with yellow and orange for accents and a bit of green.

Color palette for *Iris*

I pull a selection of purples, from light to dark, and several yellows, as well as white and black fabrics. I set aside the green fabric, unsure if I'm going to use it. This initial gathering of fabrics is comprised of 100% cottons of various weights and textures, from dotted Swiss and seersucker to sheeting.

## Trace the Shapes to Interfacing

It's easiest to trace the shape onto the interfacing first. Using a very fine permanent marker, I trace on the paper (non-adhesive) side of the iron-on interfacing. Because the *Iris* design is symmetrical, I trace each petal pattern twice, once face up and once face down.

## Back Pieces with Interfacing

Now, I'm ready to transform my chosen palette of fabrics into shapes. However, in order to make the fabric pieces sturdy enough to manipulate and withstand a lot of machine embroidery and quilting, I need to back them with iron-on interfacing.

## Cut Out the Patterns

After tracing the pattern pieces onto the interfacing, I cut them out with scissors or an X-Acto knife outside of the drawn line.

## Adhere Patterns to Fabrics

Using an iron set on steam, I adhere the interfacing patterns to the back of the appropriate fabrics. The interfacing stabilizes the grain of the fabric so I don't have to worry about it.

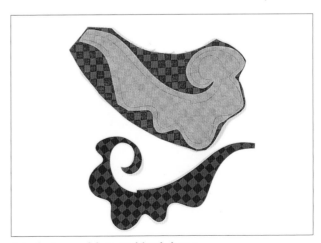

Interfacing on fabric and final shape

## Cut the Two Layers

After the interfacing has been adhered to the fabric, I cut the two layers along the traced pattern lines so the edges are as smooth and graceful as possible. I use an X-Acto knife to cut these shapes because the extra layer of interfacing gives the fabric body and I can achieve a more graceful line than with another cutting tool.

## Stand Back and Observe

After all the fabric pieces are cut, I pin them to the work wall to make sure I'm pleased with my fabric choices. If not, I try new colors until I'm satisfied. I also start thinking about the fabric that I'd like to use for the background. First, I assemble the petal units and then audition several different background fabrics.

## Assemble the Layers

Each petal of the iris is assembled one layer at a time using the petal tracings as placement guides. Flipping over the tracing so I'm looking at the reverse side, I place two neighboring pieces together, lining up the exposed edge with the corresponding line on the tracing. I use masking tape on the backside of the pieces to tack them together, being certain to put the tape where I will not sew through it.

## Sew the Petal Units Together

Using a long straight stitch of matching sturdy cotton/poly thread, I stitch the petal units together along the outside edge of the overlapping layer. I use an open-toed embroidery foot so I can easily see where the needle will land. This line of stitching is eventually covered with a satin stitch or other decorative embroidery. I remove the tape and continue this procedure until the entire petal is constructed.

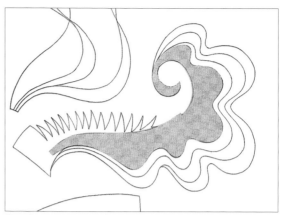

Petal construction: Step 1

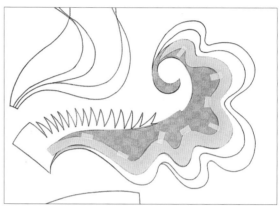

Petal construction: Step 2

Petal construction: Step 3

Petal construction: Step 4

## Play with the Design

After each petal unit is made, I pin it to the wall in the same layout as the original line drawing. I like to try some variations by shifting and tilting the petals or even totally misplacing some of them. I then use paper strips to mask the edges to test new borders and proportions.

Petal arrangement #1

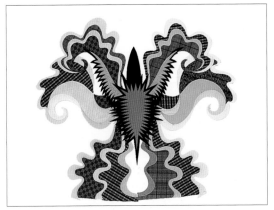

Petal arrangement #2

Petal arrangement #4

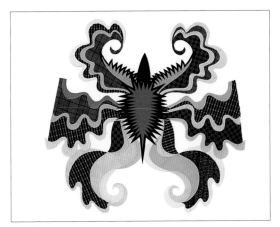

Petal arrangement #3

Petal arrangement #5

Final arrangement

Although rearranging the petals produces some interesting results, I decide to stick close to the original layout. This composition emphasizes the iris's proud posture and elegant symmetry. However, the composition still needs something; the design needs a sense of purpose, an attitude.

## Finishing Touches

Instinct tells me some long green leaves are just what this composition needs. They will provide good contrast in shape and color to the wavy purple and yellow petals. I also recall having a lot of leftover leaves from my *Trouble in the Garden* quilt (page 44) that may be worth auditioning. I unearth the four-year-old leaves from my orphaned-shapes file.

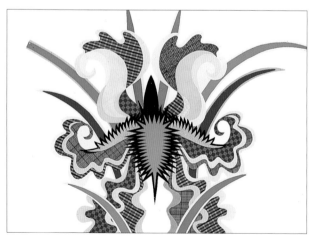

Final arrangement with leaves

Happily, they are a strong solution. The premade leaves not only mirror the shape of real iris leaves but also are the right size. Even the yellow and orange outlines add strength to the overall effect. The quilt retains its simplicity, but now it has a depth and sense of place that was missing before. The new leaves also create the impression of movement and the energy of growth.

Final arrangement with leaves and masking

Now the iris is growing in a garden or field; it isn't an isolated blossom floating in space. This sense of place is heightened when the edges are masked. Even though the ends of the petals and leaves are lost, this severe cropping concentrates the focus and actually adds energy and excitement to the composition. Somehow, we know the leaves continue beyond the frame and life goes on in the surrounding part of the picture that we don't see. Our brains fill in the implied surrounding environment. Like a close-up photograph, this becomes a slice of life, part of an isolated scene with the whole world revolving around it.

I often employ this "slice of life" editing technique in my work because it suggests the existence of a larger universe, while allowing me to focus on the earthly details. I will, of course, save the remaining leaf pieces, once they are trimmed, for potential enhancements on future quilts.

## Background Fabric

The background choice is the last fabric and color decision before I begin the embroidery. However, this is not always the case. Sometimes I begin with the background first and build the composition on top of it. I call this technique "building from the bottom up." For the *Iris* quilt, I "build from the top down" or begin with the applied units of the design and add the background last.

After observing hundreds of irises, often on spring mornings at the historic Graceland Cemetery, a peaceful oasis on the northside of Chicago, I knew I didn't want my standard stark black or white background. I wanted to use "sky" colors to suggest the fresh spring air and the energy of those proud blossoms against the clear blue sky. I suspected that baby blue would look too cute and conventional. Instead, I gather a graduated palette of odd gray blues.

The spaces between the leaves create obvious areas for each separate color to occupy. They also allow the colors to graduate easily. I attach the background fabrics the same way that the petal sections were constructed, with over- and underlapping units. In this case, I cut the background sections to lie underneath the flowers and leaves.

## Determine Background Shapes

To determine the shape for each background section, I pin a sheet of tracing paper to the wall, over the quilt. I then outline the empty spaces, allowing an extra ½" to 1" on all sides. This excess allows for slight shifts that might occur during reconstruction.

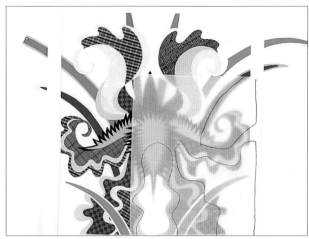

Outline empty spaces for background

## Create a Master Tracing

This is the perfect time to make a master tracing of the final composition so the individual pieces can be returned to their proper places when the background has been positioned. Having a master tracing also helps replace sections correctly after I've done some of the surface embroidery.

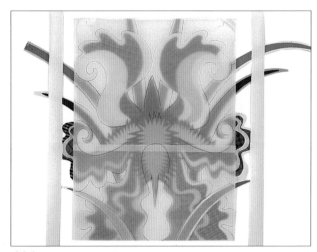

Make a master tracing

DESIGN

## Create Background Pieces

From my tracings, I cut out iron-on interfacing pieces and iron them to the backside of the appropriate background fabric. I cut the fabric along the interfacing outline and tuck the sections of background underneath the petals and leaves. All the edges of the background fabric will be hidden under the neighboring pieces. Eventually, these independent sections of petal, leaf, and background will be attached with a matching straight stitch, as with the petal sections.

## Embroider Small Pieces

Before the whole top is sewn together, I complete as much surface embroidery on small independent sections as possible. It is much easier to manipulate a small 10" unit in the sewing machine than a large quilt top. The severe curves of the iris require a lot of concentration and control.

I decide to keep the surface of the *Iris* quilt clean and simple, so I use a basic satin stitch that follows and emphasizes the wavy lines. The satin stitch covers the edges held together with the matching straight stitch. The satin stitch actually holds the entire quilt top together as well as finishes all the raw edges.

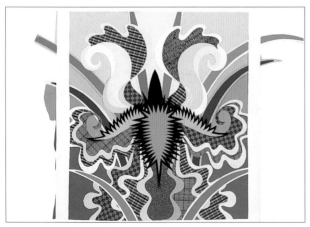

*Iris* with background in place

## THE FORMAL PROCESS IN SUMMARY

The arrangement of the petals, the addition of the leaves, and the selection of the background fabrics were all instinctual decisions. Yes, I began with an idea, even a drawing from which patterns were made, but from that point on, the arrangement, altering, adding, and editing were all decided along the way. Some of these ideas came quickly and some were painfully slow to appear. All were unexpected opportunities resulting from the creative process that must be allowed to thrive from your first sketch to your last stitch.

You must constantly select and edit to give your work its full potential. Allow yourself time to make these decisions and discoveries, for each of them will contribute positively to the finished work.

# MACHINE EMBROIDERY: THE IMPORTANCE OF CRAFTSMANSHIP

Every step of the quiltmaking process builds new layers of detail and strength to the final artwork and, as with every step, embroidery is a crucial design element. Minor details in embroidery can contribute major differences to the finished work.

Embroidery should enhance the design and exploit the unique characteristics of thread.

The stitches should look like embroidery. They should be a purposeful improvement to the visual design and the emotional intent of the work, as opposed to being superfluous and fussy. Consequently, embroidery needs to be conscientiously and intelligently applied. It takes the same thoughtful consideration that is given to designing, choosing colors, and arranging elements.

Embroidery should look as if it was effortlessly applied, an effect that only comes through with a high level of craftsmanship. This is especially true for work as graphic as mine. Any imperfection in the stitching is quite obvious and detracts from the overall impact of the work.

It's important that my skills as a craftsperson contribute to my work, not detract from it. I don't want to be at the mercy of a difficult technique or torture myself, my machine, or my materials. Elements should work together to benefit the final product. All quilt artists must recognize their own skills, their abilities, and their limitations, and work within that structure. You must learn to apply your abilities to their greatest benefit.

▼ Detail of *Memory Garden*.
Photo by Judy Smith-Kressley.

▲ Detail of *Sun Flowers*.
Photo by Gregory Gantner.

ERY

◄ Detail of *Crystal Garden.*

▼ Detail of *Thorn Garden.*

*Photos by Gregory Gantner.*

▲ Detail of *Tree of Life: Summer.*

► Detail of *Willow.*

*Photos by Gregory Gantner.*

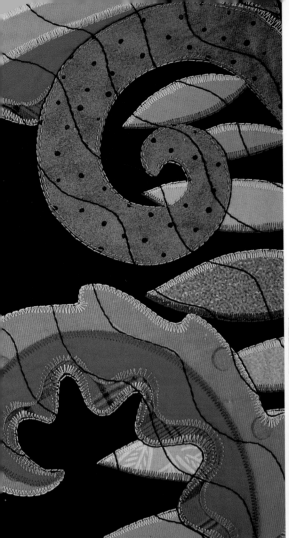

With patience and practice, all skills, both natural and newly acquired, are improvable. Therefore, it's important to have a practical understanding of the techniques and the craftsmanship involved. It is important to practice your embroidery skills if embroidery is a necessary part of your creative expression. You can't expect that, simply because you understand the method of working, you will be able to achieve perfect results on the first attempt. Practice is essential for perfecting craftsmanship and strengthening your artistic artillery.

◄ Detail of *Lily*.
▼ Detail of *Willow's Weeds*.
*Photos by Gregory Gantner.*

▲ Detail of *Brambles*.
*Photo by Gregory Gantner.*

▶ Detail of *Visitation*.
*Photo by Judy Smith-Kressley.*

◀ Detail of *Crown of Thorns*.
*Photo by Gregory Gantner.*

◀ Detail of *Curl I*.
▼ Detail of *Seeds and Blossoms*.
*Photos by Gregory Gantner.*

▲ Detail of *Resurrection*.
*Photo by Gregory Gantner.*

▶ Detail of *Seeds*.
*Photo by Judy Smith-Kressley.*

Patience is the other essential quality that must be cultivated for improving your craftsmanship. Very few machine embroidery techniques can be mastered successfully with your "pedal to the metal." Mastery of machine embroidery is achieved with slow and deliberate stitching. You must practice your technique until you are able to control both your fabric and your sewing machine simultaneously.

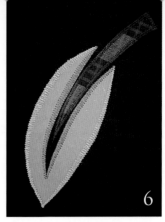

# SATIN STITCH

There are actually very few stitches on my fancy sewing machine that are appropriate for my hard-edged graphic style; however, the satin stitch is one I have come to rely on for its simplicity and versatility.

I use the satin stitch to cover the raw edges of my raw-edged appliquéd shapes and to attach two overlapping pattern pieces. This means that the satin stitch line often follows or outlines each individual shape and pattern piece.

Satin stitch is just a fancy name for the zigzag stitch. By adjusting the length and width of the stitch, I can take advantage of many design effects. I've discovered that this simple stitch can enhance the quilt's surface by either defining or distorting the shapes and lines of the design. The satin stitch can electrify, or it can subtly blend shapes and colors.

The satin stitch can also act as a drawing line, which becomes a new graphic element all together. I especially enjoy using this stitch in a painterly way to suggest the presence of a light source, such as the sun, and as a sculpting tool to give the illusion of depth and texture to the surface.

1. Satin stitch using matching thread to define

2. Satin stitch to distort the shape

3. Satin stitch to draw a line

4. Satin stitch using contrasting thread to add intensity

5 & 6. Satin stitch to create dimension

## Defining Shapes

To reinforce and emphasize the line between the leaf and the background, I use matching thread and a slightly open satin stitch so the fabric of the leaf is still visible. The needle follows the edge of the leaf as its guide.

## Blurring or Distorting Shapes

A neighboring color of thread is used with a slightly open satin stitch. The stitch overlaps both the leaf's perimeter and the black background to blur or distort the definite silhouette of the leaf.

## As a Drawing Line

A tight or closed satin stitch creates a solid line of color. This line is so strong and definite that it adds a whole new design element to the quilt. It also creates additional texture and interest because of the raised thread on the fabric's surface.

## Electrifying Shapes

A contrasting color of shiny rayon thread makes the leaf seem to glow and vibrate. This effect adds vitality and enlivens the quilt design.

## Painting and Sculpting Shapes

The existence of sunlight is implied because this leaf is outlined with light and shadow. Use of a lighter thread on one side and a darker thread on the other creates the illusion of dimension and depth.

It is also important that you allow yourself time to complete the embroidery stage to the best advantage of the work. At times, machine embroidery and quilting can be exhausting and monotonous due to the intense concentration required and the tedious repetition of tasks. However, there is a difference between what is monotonous while working and what is monotonous to look at in the finished quilt.

Each stitch should strengthen the visual impact of the quilt. Some stitches will be obvious and easy to see, but some important stitching can be so subtle and subliminal, that the viewer only sees the impact or effect, but is unaware of its existence.

Quilters must learn to weigh the desired visual effect of their work and the time they devote to it. Devoting the necessary time to your work will make it sing. Sometimes less is more when it comes to applying embroidery; sometimes more is better. The trick is letting each successive layer of attention contribute to strengthening the voice of the final work.

To relieve the strain and tedium of the embroidery and quilting phase, I try to vary my tasks from time to time and to allow myself frequent breaks. It's helpful to find small diversions so you can maintain your enthusiasm for the job. Wash a few dishes, see what's new (or old) in the refrigerator, or sweep the floor. These tasks will definitely make returning to tedious embroidery look good by comparison. Listening to books-on-tape is also a wonderful way to keep your thinking mind occupied while you work on automated tasks.

When the quilt is finished, tedious tasks, such as embroidery and quilting, should not look tedious and strained. They should look effortless and painlessly integrated into the whole design. Your diligent attention should manifest itself into delicious details that accentuate and energize your quilt.

On each of the leaf samples, I used an open-toed embroidery foot on my sewing machine, which allows me to see the stitches as they are being made and to guide the needle with more precision. The threads are basic cotton/poly or a 30 weight rayon, both with cotton/poly thread in the bobbin. I also adjusted the width of the satin stitch to accentuate the points and curves of the leaf. The stitch is narrow at the base and gradually widens as the leaf widens. At the mid-point, the stitch begins to taper toward the tip of the leaf.

## OTHER EMBROIDERY OPTIONS

Each quilter has a different style of working and individual ideas to express. Just as quilters are different, so are sewing machines. Each brand and model offers a unique selection of features and stitches. Quilters must discover for themselves which machine, features, and stitches are appropriate for their work.

Most of us are limited to the machine we already have and should, therefore, learn to explore its abilities to our fullest advantage. I have a pretty fancy sewing machine with many stitches and features, but even so, there are very few stitches that are appropriate for my visual style. Occasionally, I'm thrilled to discover a new stitch that can speak my language. Each of these stitches becomes part of my visual vocabulary.

To test the stitches and effects of your own machine, I suggest that you make a sampler such as the one shown on the next page. Apply simple shapes, such as leaves or doughnuts, with fusible web to a solid-colored background. I also recommend reinforcing your background fabric with a layer of interfacing or tear-away stabilizer to keep your sampler from buckling.

Now try as many stitches and variations as your machine will perform. Some stitches will look better than others. Some will look good but will be inappropriate for your style of work. Occasionally, however, a stitch surprises you by being the perfect finish you've been looking for. This is also a good way to practice your embroidery skills.

# QUILTING

Traditionally, a quilt is made of a three-layer sandwich: the decorative layer or quilt top, the batting or thin sheet of cotton or polyester padding, and the backing. To hold these layers together, the quilt must be stitched through all three layers at the same time. All of my quilts are machine quilted. This is a necessity because I use a lot of heavy fabrics, which are usually lined with interfacing, and require the machine's strength to penetrate the layers.

My quilting designs are of three styles. One style simply follows the shapes inside the design, as with the *Iris* quilt. Another style is an all-over pattern of wavy lines, as with the *Weeds* quilt. Sometimes, I use a more decorative stitch to fill the background, as with the *Bandana* quilt.

The quilting design is not determined until the top is finished. If the quilting lines follow the design of the quilt top, I usually "eyeball" the stitching and no marking is necessary. However, if the quilting cuts through the design, as in the case of an all-over pattern of wavy quilting, I mark the stitching path, lightly, with a pencil. Over the years, I have made many sizes of wiggly templates, each made with standard template plastic and cut with an X-Acto knife. The curve on each side is the same, like a wavy ruler. This allows the template to fit perfectly beside the previously drawn lines and repeat at regular intervals. I use soft colored pencils, such as Prismacolor®, to faintly trace the quilting pattern. Over time, this pencil line simply disappears.

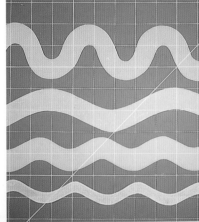

Wavy quilting templates

▲ Detail of *Weeds*.
*Photo by Gregory Gantner.*

◄ Detail of *Tree of Life: Bandana*.
*Photo by Judy Smith-Kressley.*

▲ Detail of *Iris*.
*Photo by Judy Smith-Kressley.*

Currently, I favor using top-stitching thread for all quilting, with cotton/poly in the bobbin. I use a combination of walking foot and open-toed embroidery foot for quilting. Top-stitching thread is heavy and makes a delicious and definite line that adds texture and interest to the flat surface of a quilt.

Back of *Iris* showing quilting lines.
*Photo by Judy Smith-Kressley.*

Quilting is not a speedy process. Practice and patience are needed to master the mechanics of machine quilting. It usually takes as long for me to quilt a piece as it does to construct the top. I can only machine quilt for a short time before I have

to stop to pull all the loose threads to the back of the quilt for tying and burying. I use a self-threading needle to bury threads. A self-threading needle does not require that you poke the thread through a small eye. Instead, the thread snaps into the eye through a small V-shaped channel at the end of the needle. This saves a lot of time and frustration. However, all self-threading needles are not created equally; be sure to test each needle before use. Check that your needle doesn't break or fray your thread. A good self-threading needle is precious and should be stored in a safe place.

Although quilting is the final phase in an intense process, you must be willing to give quilting as much attention as designing and construction. Quilting adds the final layer of depth and detail to the surface of your design. Your choices should be considered thoughtfully.

As I work, I try to please and surprise myself by discovering new combinations of shapes and colors. I try to listen to the quilt and respond to its demands. I attempt to make a precious object, so I work to the best of my ability throughout each step of the process. My abilities and standards change as I add and subtract techniques and images.

By the time a quilt is finished and ready to leave home, it has been infused with passion and attention. It has been empowered a layer at a time, each detail thoroughly addressed. When it travels into the world, it carries that energy with it. A quilt must convey its message without me. When it's finished, I stitch my name onto the back. After that, it's on its own. I cut it loose and move on to the next one.

A successful quilt radiates energy; it also absorbs new energy as it travels and feeds it back to me. We exchange gifts. I use my talent and passion to make the quilt and the quilt becomes my ambassador, my voice. Selling a quilt is part of this energy exchange. The sale completes the cycle. The quilt has generated enough interest and vitality to attract someone's attention, and that someone is willing to trade his or her own gift in return. It is a high compliment to sell a piece. I love having passionate collectors because I know my quilts will go to good homes.

The quilts also create an exchange of energy in the classroom. They share their secrets with receptive students and hopefully their enthusiasm is contagious. The classroom is where I get direct feedback from my work. Plus, the students inspire me with new color combinations and great new shapes so that I can barely wait to get back to my studio and play.

It's a simple life of inspiration and perspiration, of hard work and wonderful rewards. I am so thankful to be able to do what I love: to play with line, color, shape, and texture; to create with fabric and thread; to use my head, my heart, and my hands. It's a wonderful life! Let's celebrate!

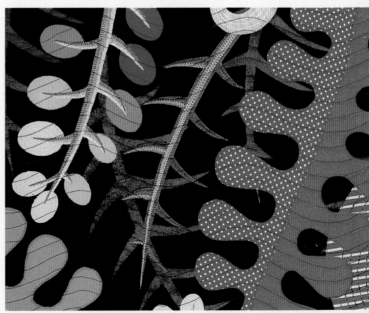

▲ Detail of *Color Garden*.
Photo by Gregory Gantner.

# OTHER FINE BOOKS FROM C&T PUBLISHING

For more information write for a free catalog:
C&T Publishing, Inc.
P.O. Box 1456
Lafayette, CA 94549
(800) 284-1114
e-mail: ctinfo@ctpub.com
http://www.ctpub.com

For quilting supplies:
Cotton Patch Mail Order
3405 Brown Avenue, Dept. CTB
Lafayette, CA 94549
e-mail: quiltusa@yahoo.com
http://www.quiltusa.com
(800) 835-4418
(925) 283-7883

# SUGGESTED READING

Ackerman, Diane. *A Natural History of the Senses.* New York: Random House, Inc., 1990.

Adam, Hans Christian. *Karl Blossfeldt 1865-1932.* Kuln, London, Madrid, New York, Paris, Tokyo: Taschen, 1999.

Bossert, Helmuth *The Folk Art of Asia, Africa and the Americas.* New York: Hastings House, Publishers, 1977. Original published in 1924.

Bossert, Helmuth *The Folk Art of Europe.* New York: Hastings House, Publishers, 1977. Original published in 1924.

Bossert, Helmuth *The Peasant Art of Europe and Asia.* New York: Hastings House, Publishers, 1977. Original published in 1924.

Cliff, Stafford. *The English Archive of Design and Decoration.* New York: Harry N. Abrams, Inc., Publishers, 1998.

Day, Lewis F. *Pattern Design.* New York: Taplinger Publishing Company, 1979. Original published in 1903.

Durant, Stuart. *Ornament: From the Industrial Revolution to Today.* Woodstock, New York: The Overlook Press, 1986.

Gere, Charlotte and Michael Whiteway. *Nineteenth Century Design: From Pugin to Mackintosh.* New York: Harry N. Abrams, Inc., Publishers, 1994.

Haeckel, Ernst. *Art Forms in Nature.* Munich, New York: Prestel-Verlag, 1998.

Hatton, Richard. *Handbook of Plant and Floral Ornament from Early Herbals.* New York: Dover Publications, Inc., 1960. Originally published in 1909 under the title, *The Craftsman's Plant Book.*

Jensen, Robert and Patricia Conway. *Ornamentalism: The New Decorativeness in Architecture and Design.* New York: Clarkson N. Potter, Inc., Publishers, 1982.

Jones, Owen. *The Grammar of Ornament.* New York: Van Nostrand Reinhold Company, 1982. Originally published in 1856.

MacKown, Diana. *Dawns and Dusks.* New York: Charles Scribner's Sons, 1976.

Kahr, Joan. *Edgar Brandt: Master of Art Deco Ironwork.* New York: Harry N. Abrams, Inc., Publishers, 1999.

# INDEX

## The Quilts

Bold page numbers denote quilt detail.

Matsuya Piece-Goods Store. *Japanese Design Motifs: 4260 Illustrations of Heraldic Crests*. New York: Dover Publications, Inc., 1972. Originally published in 1913.

Meyer, Franz Sales. *Handbook of Ornament*. New York: Dover Publications, 1957. Originally published in 1888.

Nordness, Lee. *Objects USA*. New York: The Viking Press, 1970.

Paine, Sheila. *Embroidered Textiles: Traditional Patterns from Five Continents*. London: Thames and Hudson Ltd., 1990.

Racinet, Albert. *The Encyclopedia of Ornamant*. New York: Portland House, 1988. Originally published in 1873 as Polychromatic Ornament.

## MAGAZINES

*American Craft*. American Craft Council, 72 Spring Street, New York, 10012-4019. To subscribe, call (800) 562-1973.

*Art and Antiques*. Trans World Publishing, Inc., 3 East 54th Street, New York, 10022.

*Art/Quilt Magazine*, P.O. Box 630927, Houston, TX 77263-0927 (800) 399-3532.

*Crafts, The British Applied and Decorative Arts Magazine*, c/o Mercury Airfreight Int. Ltd., 365 Blair Rd., Ave. 1, NJ 07001.

*FIBERARTS: The Magazine of Textiles*. Altamont Press, 50 College Street, Asheville, North Carolina, 28801. To subscribe, call (800) 284-3388.

*Garden Design*. Meigher Communications, LP., 100 Avenue of the Americas New York, 10013-1605.

*Gardens Illustrated*. John Brown Publishing Ltd., The Boathouse, Crabtree Lane, London SW6 6LU.

*Hali*, St. Giles House, 50 Poland St., London, W1V 4AX, +44 (0) 1858 438818. e-mail: hali@centaur.co.uk.

*Ornament: The Art of Personal Adornments*. Published by Carolyn L.E. Benesh and Robert K. Liu, P.O. Box 2349, San Marcos, CA 92079-2349.

*PIECEWORK*. Published by Interweave Press. 201 E. Fourth St., Loveland, CO 80537. (800) 645-3675. To subscribe call (800) 340-7496.

*Metalsmith*. Published by the Society of North American Goldsmiths (SNAG), 2275 Amigo Drive, Missoula, MT 59808, (406) 728-5248. To subscribe, call (630) 579-3272 (the SNAG/Metalsmith Business Office).

# ABOUT THE AUTHOR

Jane A. Sassaman studied textile and jewelry design at Iowa State University. After graduating, she worked as a window dresser, an illustrator, and a designer of decorative accessories while actively searching for her means of expression. In 1980 she discovered art quilts and she knew the search was over. Quilting satisfied the artist, the craftsman, and the draftsman in her—using her heart, head, and hands. Since then, she has devoted herself to quilting. Through her twenty year career, Jane has developed a distinguished style. Her work is exuberant, colorful, and vividly graphic. The quilts celebrate the wonders of the natural world and dance with energy and movement.

Jane's quilts are shown worldwide and can be found in many private and corporate art collections. Her quilt *Willow* was named one of the best 100 American Quilts of the Century. She was awarded the Quilts Japan Award for her work in Quilt National 1999. She also received "The Fairfield Master Award for Contemporary Artistry" at the International Quilt Festival in 1996. Jane lives in Chicago with her husband and two children.